ARCHETYPAL AND CULTURAL PERSPECTIVES ON THE FOREIGNER

In this era of intense migration, the topic of the foreigner is of paramount importance. Joanne Wieland-Burston examines the question of the "foreign" and "foreigner" from multiple perspectives and explores how Jung and Freud were more interested in the wide phenomenon of the foreign in the unconscious rather than in their own personal lives. She analyses cultural approaches to the archetype of the foreigner throughout history using literary, cultural (as seen in mythological texts and fairy tales) and psychological references, and interprets the scapegoating of foreign minorities as a projection of the monster onto the foreigner. The book includes contemporary perspectives on immigration and displacement throughout, from analysing patient case material, the archetypal needs of people who join terrorist groups, feelings of alienation, and the work of Palestinian-German psychologist Ahmad Mansour. Throughout this personal and highly topical study, Wieland questions and studies C. G. Jung's own reflections on himself as a foreigner and her own personal experiences.

This book will be vital reading for Jungian psychotherapists and analytical psychologists in practice and in training, as well as for academics and students of Jungian and post-Jungian studies, archetypal studies, identity politics, and courses examining the experiences of displaced persons, refugees, migrants and minority groups.

Joanne Wieland-Burston is an American-born Jungian analyst who studied in Zurich, Switzerland (1977–1981) and presently practises in Munich, Germany. She is a training analyst, supervisor and instructor at the International School for Analytical Psychology in Zurich and lectures internationally. Her background is in literature and art history.

"Joanne Wieland-Burston offers us a book that is quite clear, profound, and excellently documented, on our relationship with the foreigner within us, around us, and afar. It provides observation, investigation, analysis, and personal experience that are of practical use to psychoanalysts and psycho-therapists, researchers in the social sciences, and each one of us."

Christian Gaillard, Dr. Psy., training psychoanalyst and supervisor, former President of the International Association for Analytical Psychology, former Professor at the National Academy of Fine Arts, Paris, and author of *The Soul of Art: Analysis and Creation*, Texas AM University Press

"In this impressive and thoughtful book, Joanne Wieland-Burston helps us come to terms with the 'other' in ourselves and in the world around us. This is a most timely and useful book, full of essential insights into the times we live in."

Murray Stein, PhD, author of *Jung's Map of the Soul*

"Joanne Wieland-Burston having been herself involved with migration and alienation explores the theme of the foreigner from manifold angles based on her background as a Jungian analyst and her studies in literature and art history. Her fascinating and differentiated work centers mainly on the modern faces of the foreigner. Giving deep insight in the dominant topic of our culture she deals with the archetypal roots, cultural complexes, scape-goating, alienation of the self and brings all the aspects down to the practical work in psychotherapy. A truly wonderful and inspiring book!"

Kathrin Asper, PhD, supervisor, training analyst and lecturer at ISAPZURICH

ARCHETYPAL AND CULTURAL PERSPECTIVES ON THE FOREIGNER

Minorities and Monsters

Joanne Wieland-Burston

Routledge
Taylor & Francis Group

LONDON AND NEW YORK

First published 2020
by Routledge
2 Park Square, Milton Park, Abingdon, Oxon OX14 4RN

and by Routledge
52 Vanderbilt Avenue, New York, NY 10017

Routledge is an imprint of the Taylor & Francis Group, an informa business

© 2020 Joanne Wieland-Burston

British Library Cataloguing-in-Publication Data
A catalogue record for this book is available from the British Library

Library of Congress Cataloging-in-Publication Data
A catalog record has been requested for this book

ISBN: 978-1-138-34580-5 (hbk)
ISBN: 978-1-138-34581-2 (pbk)
ISBN: 978-0-429-43765-6 (ebk)

Typeset in Bembo
by Swales & Willis, Exeter, Devon, UK

CONTENTS

FIGURES

PREFACE

On preparing this book for publication I came to realise that I have been involved with the topic since early childhood. This has to do with the situation of the family I come from and my own migratory past. I will describe my personal relationship to the topic of the foreigner in the introduction to this book.

As a Jungian analyst in training I had to deal with the multifaceted attitude of C. G. Jung toward foreigners. Some of his remarks (those on Jewish people) I found deeply upsetting; his personal situation as a foreigner I find it easier to empathise with. And I do wonder the extent to which many aspects of Jung's theoretical work were influenced by his own extremely disturbing experiences of feeling like a foreigner. As we shall see in the following pages, the man Carl Gustav Jung plainly shows to the interested researcher many different ways of experiencing and appreciating the foreign.

Throughout my years in clinical practice I have found the topic fascinating – on many levels. So many of my clients have had to deal with feelings of alienation, many of them themselves expats or children of immigrants. Some have been, or felt like, outsiders in their own society – being nerds, homosexuals, overweight, or just in some way different from the others. I have approached the topic from various angles in many lectures in the past ten years.

In the meantime, innumerable politicians, lawyers, writers, philosophers, psychologists and sociologists have devoted so much time and energy to the phenomenon of the foreign in society that it has become a dominant topic in contemporary culture.

My perspective is that of a Jungian analyst with a background in literature and art history and a deeply concerned foreigner.

For myself the ever repeated encounters with my situation as a foreigner, with my own foreignness within has often been painful, sometimes hardly bearably so. But, coming to accept it as a fact, a matter of fact that is so intimately part of my identity, has made the situation not only easier to bear; it has become a koan for my life.

INTRODUCTION

The archetypal experience then and now

Encounters with foreigners are what we call "archetypal experiences". The Hebrew Bible is full of stories of such encounters, from Avram and Sarai's encounter with the strangers who prove to be angels, to Moses' experience as a foreigner, to the 40-year-long wanderings of the Hebrew tribes through foreign lands.

At the present time – the first quarter of the twenty-first century – the topic of the foreigner is so omnipresent that it is extremely difficult to write about it. Most of the questions and excitement revolve around immigrants and their integration in society. These people are refugees from political turmoil, people fleeing poverty and seeking a better future for themselves and their children; they are often of different cultural and religious backgrounds and may have a different skin colour from the local population. It is in this context that the political discourse has become more focused on the topics of racism and anti-Semitism. The literature abounds – from articles in the media to erudite essays and even plays and novels.

The question of the integration and, too often, of the exclusion of these foreigners is of burning interest. In some countries recent economic developments have led to new and unusual policies toward foreigners. On the positive side we see, for example, Japan whose ex-patriot population used to be relatively small and closed off from the rest of Japanese society. Low birth rates and an ageing population have caused the government to change its policy: Japan has opened up and welcomes refugees and ever more foreign workers. China is also an interesting example: the Great Wall, built to keep out the foreign invaders (and foreigners in general) has become a tourist attraction. During the Nazi period, China showed an unusual openness to Jewish refugees at a time in which the borders of most other countries were closed to them. At the present time the Chinese government officially endorses the influx of foreigners, welcomed for what they can contribute to the knowledge and advancement of the Chinese economy. Similarly, Chinese students are encouraged to travel and study in foreign countries in order to bring back newly acquired knowledge to their homeland. At the same time, however, the Uyghur people, an ethnic minority, most of whom are Muslims living in the north of China, are being sent to so-called "re-education camps". The background: over 90 per cent of the Chinese population is Han Chinese. They represent the in-group.

The situation of the United States, the classical country of immigration, which throughout its history has known quotas for foreigners, is now in an uproar with anti-Latino and anti-Muslim policies put in place by a president, provoked by his own racism, economic considerations and the traumatic repercussions of the attack on the World Trade Center by followers of Al-Qaeda.

It is all too apparent that the cohesion of the European Union and even most recently of the United States (where a group in California is threatening to secede) is being threatened in a serious way by xenophobic waves – from Trump and his border wall to East Germany's PEGIDA (Patriotic Europeans against the Islamisation of the Occident). Germany's reunification meant, among other things, having to incorporate into a relatively new democracy a society that had never known democracy. The difficulties in the new East German states manifest most poignantly and most aggressively in the extreme xenophobia rampant there. What serves as a scapegoat is a tiny minority population: relatively few refugees of Muslim origin live in the East of Germany; nevertheless, PEGIDA attempts to spread its prejudice against Islam throughout Germany with various forms of propaganda, weekly demonstrations and a newly founded anti-immigrant political party called the AfD (Alternative for Deutschland).

And the rest of Europe? A majority of Brexit supporters is motivated by the fear of an overabundance of foreign immigrants; the eastern European countries are refusing to accept immigrants. The example of France's recent legislation, which in the meantime has been declared unconstitutional, is astonishing. French citizens were being arrested and fined for helping immigrants. We are far from the ancient concept of the rights of the foreigner here.

This is the kind of prejudice and extreme nationalism we are faced with today. In his 2016 book *Strangers at our Door* Zygmunt Bauman, Professor Emeritus of Sociology at the University of Leeds, adopts the expression "migration panic" (Bauman, 2016: 1ff.) to describe the present-day atmosphere with regard to immigration; the terminology hardly seems to be an exaggeration.

Xenophobia can be seen as a phenomenon expressing the collective unconscious. It seems as though in these times of relative peace, the world is getting bored with the stasis and reverts to the enemy-seeking mentality of the past. If the wars will be fought on a large scale physically or not remains to be seen, but the ancient, traditionalist "we versus them" mentality definitely counteracts stasis. In a time when witches are normally no longer the preferred scapegoats (as had been the case mainly in the Middle Ages, but up until the eighteenth century and sometimes beyond), others are found and attacked, if not physically – which sometimes does happen – at least verbally and ideologically. That is why it is absolutely urgent for people from various fields to try to understand the nationalism and accompanying xenophobia and identity crisis that have gripped our world, and the dangerous dynamics hence in play against the numerous foreigners of our day.

I will be examining here mainly modern faces of the foreigner, but not without referring to more ancient faces of foreigners and attitudes toward them.

Jung and Freud's stance on the foreign

As a Jungian analyst I am necessarily also interested in the way in which C. G. Jung dealt with the foreign in his own life and how he theorised on the subject.

In his autobiography, Jung seems to be mainly fascinated by the foreign beings who arose from his own unconscious, first of all by Philemon. From what we read in Jung's works, the question of the foreignness of his clientele was not a major concern. It is seldom if ever mentioned. Jung's focus was more on the unconscious of humanity as a whole, the collective unconscious, not the layer of the collective unconscious that is formed through national, religious or ethnic culture. We contemporary Jungians are more interested in the latter today and refer to this layer as cultural complexes. Jung reports on his travels to foreign, exotic countries such as India and the African continent where he observes rituals, which offer him proof of the existence of the collective unconscious. The so-called "primitives" fascinated him; the term was common at that time, not meant in a degrading manner but part of the unthinking colonial attitude. This attitude is also evidenced in the fact that it was common, "normal" even, to exhibit African tribes in zoos in Europe, but also in the US up until the middle of the twentieth century. Jung may have even gone to the Basle Zoo in 1935 to see the "*Völk-erschau*" (a people show) of an African tribe.

Jung's essay on the characteristics of the Jewish people is a clear, if rather helpless effort to define the foreignness of Jews in a way that history will never forget. Interestingly enough, Erich Neumann himself also approached the topic in an unpublished manuscript of several hundred pages called *Beiträge zur Tiefenpsychologie des jüdischen Menschen und zum Problem der Offenbarung* (*A Contribution to the Psychology of the Jewish People and to the Revelation*), which he wrote in the 1930s: he dated it 1938, but decided never to publish because of the political situation of the times.

Many foreigners came to consult Jung, mostly Americans, but also Europeans. In her biography, Deidre Bair is quite adamant in her insistence that, for example, Sabina Spielrein "represented the wildness of all that was foreign" for Jung, that she radiated "an air of exoticism" and hence, Jung was "intrigued by her as a woman because she was unlike any he had known thus far". He was, according to Deidre Bair, fascinated by this "so very foreign being" (Bair, 2003: 91). But the foreignness of his clientele is not a topic on which Jung seems to dwell or on which he shows any kind of scientific interest.

One could imagine another, more personal aspect of the topic of foreignness in Jung's life, which he himself, however, mentions only briefly in his autobiography. Although he was Swiss, Jung was a foreigner in Zurich. After completing his studies in Basel he went to work at the Burghölzli Clinic in Zurich. The extent to which a Swiss person from Basel could then and to a certain degree still now can be considered a foreigner in Zurich must not be underestimated; this was especially so in Jung's time. There are very pronounced cultural, social and linguistic differences between these two cities, although both belong to the German part of Switzerland. Competition between the two cities has always been lively, with prejudices abounding. Jung was quite aware of the difference between the two cities, as he states in his autobiography (Jung, 1962: 136), but he rather felt that the move offered him a new kind of freedom; he felt he could escape there from being stamped as the son of Reverend Jung and the grandson of Professor Jung. On the level of social class Jung, I must add, was also a foreigner – to his wife's social class. We do not learn of any discomfort he may have felt about this difference in social class nor about his being a Basler in the city of Zurich. It seems that this aspect of his identity was not important to him. At least he had a Protestant background like the majority of inhabitants of the canton.

But there is a much more intimate level of his feeling of foreignness to which, as an old man, Jung admits in his autobiography. Here he reveals that from an early age he felt like a foreigner. As a child he felt lonely because of his dreams and then as an adult because of his work with his unconscious. He felt foreign in the world outside, and later in his inner world and speaks of "the alienation which so long separated me from the world" (Jung, 1962: 419). He mentions that whenever he spoke to people about his inner world he felt like a foreigner. He names this feeling his "old wound, the feeling of being an outsider and of alienating others" and felt it especially intensely when he decided to become a psychiatrist (Jung, 1962: 134). But he persisted, nonetheless, because he was fascinated by the idea of studying "the pathological variants of so-called normality", hoping that they would help him achieve "a deeper insight into the psyche" (probably his own!) (Jung, 1962: 137).

After his break with Freud, flooded by his unconscious, Jung admits to his helplessness, faced with a foreign and incomprehensible world. That he did not break, as others had before him (he mentions Nietzsche and Hölderlin), he attributes to a demonic strength. He was determined to try to understand the meaning of what was happening to him.

One can surmise that one intense personal motivation for going beyond Freud's concept of the personal unconscious was a yearning for community, for a sense of belonging to the rest of humanity, no longer feeling like a foreigner, an outsider, but sharing typically human problems and typically human motifs and motives.

Jung's concepts of the shadow, the Self and individuation are based on these personal experiences of feeling foreign, different. In trying to deal with the foreign, which he discovered within, he seems to have been motivated, at least in part, by the need to find a larger framework, an ordering system that could encompass and explain his chaotic adventures in his inner world, which otherwise could too easily have led to exclusion from society. Many have called Jung's dreams and visions (which he recorded in words and images in *The Red Book*) after his separation from master and father figure Freud, psychotic. Thanks to the concepts, which he developed on the basis of his own experience, Jung was able to order these experiences, placing them in the context of a whole, seeing them as signs of his individuality and at the same time signs of his inclusion in humanity as a whole.

Freud, too, was a foreigner, and he was painfully aware of this fact. He did not share the same religious background of the city in which he worked and lived. Nor was he a native of Vienna either: his family came from a small town in the Austrian Republic and moved to Vienna when he was four years old. The rural area he had spent his early years in was extremely different from the cultural centre, which Vienna was at the time. In some way, the little boy Freud can be considered "a country bumpkin" in the big city. But, this is not what seems to have preoccupied him the most. Freud's feeling foreign as a Jew is apparent in all of his work; it is also more than apparent in his need to choose Jung, a Christian, as his "*prince héritier*", his official representative of psychoanalysis. Otherwise psychoanalysis would continue to be seen as the "Jewish science".

For Jung, as for Freud, their main interest was definitely the fascinating foreignness of the unconscious. Learning to shine light on, to get acquainted with and to understand this thus far strange and foreign domain was their goal. Perhaps finding a sense of familiarity with the unconscious was more feasible for Freud than for Jung who, with his concept of the collective unconscious, granted that domain a never-ending sense of mystery.

But, for neither man, both actually foreigners, was the question of their own foreignness an aspect of their identity to which they decided to devote their scientific attention. This was not their focus. In our day and age our perspective on such questions has changed. The topic of identity has, like that of cultural complexes, become important for us. Immigration, in Jung and Freud's time, was largely from Europe to the United States and primarily (before the Nazi period) because of poverty. The immigrant populations then were neither as large nor as diverse as today.

Who is interested today?

Apart from contemporary politicians, those who in the past 50 years have devoted the most time and energy to the foreigner and related topics were and are themselves foreigners: Marcel Camus, Emmanuel Levinas, Julia Kristeva, Jacques Derrida and, more recently, Charles Taylor and Kwame Anthony Appiah, to mention just a few. And so, it should not surprise the reader that I also devote myself to the topic, which has been so central in my life.

My personal interest

As my clientele tends to have had international backgrounds, I have been in touch with the foreigner's point of view through my analytic work. While preparing this manuscript, I came to realise that the topic of foreignness – my own and that of others – has actually been the background of my life from the beginning. And it is probably the reason I became an analyst. My earliest conscious memory of feeling like a foreigner dates from 1950. I was five years old when my family moved from North Carolina to Boston. Sitting on the grass near our new apartment with my new friends one said, "Joanne, you talk so funny!". I can still hear this today as I sit writing at my desk in my Munich apartment. At that time, I could not understand this remark at all. Now I know that I must have had a very typically Southern accent, a so-called "Southern Drawl", but for me at that moment, I thought something quite different and so I answered, "But, you talk so funny!". I was new in Boston; I was the foreigner.

In fact this situation was part of my life from the beginning. I was born in North Carolina – my father had been transferred there for work. Neither of my parents came from the South. We remained there five years as outsiders to a well-established community. According to my parents' stories, they felt excluded. I was too young to feel it consciously.

What I did notice and feel consciously was the way that Black people were treated at that time in the still very segregated South. They were considered outsiders, not belonging and inferior. I remember how the bus driver yelled to a Black lady – Blacks were called "coloured" at that time – "Get to the back of the bus!"; but the lady couldn't: the bus was too crowded. The driver threw her off the bus. I was four or five years old and worried that it was late and that the lady would not be able to get home. Other early memories of segregation were in restaurants, ice cream parlours and lunch counters; I could not see any Black people anywhere nearby: I would find them later, in completely separate parts of the restaurant or the counter. These precocious encounters with the exclusion of foreigners disturbed me deeply as a small child.

We left North Carolina for Boston because of my father's work. Here I went to school; here I felt at home. My family belonged to the in-group, not like the families who lived across the street in the "Project", a complex of apartments built for poor people. Our side of the street was for the middle-class families who had moved in before the "Project" was built. This differentiation was plain and clear. I did not feel comfortable with it and despite my mother's complaints I became friends with kids from school who lived in the "Project".

We left Boston after eight years because my father was denied a well-earned promotion in his government job (according to his boss who wrote to inform him of the decision and the reason for it) because he was Jewish. This I did not know as a 13-year-old child and actually only discovered it when my father died and I read some documents that he had saved.

The next stop was Los Angeles where my father struggled to find a job, but ultimately accomplished it. For a teenager brought up on the

East coast of the US, the West coast created an extreme feeling of "dépaysement". It didn't feel like I belonged at all: school mates had big, beautiful houses with swimming pools; getting good grades was easy here in comparison with my two years at Girls' Latin school in Boston. We saw famous actors and actresses on the streets; I never felt I belonged there, but Los Angeles' differentness was somehow exciting.

The California stint was short – one and a half years – and then, off to Toronto, Canada where my father had been offered a better job. As an American kid in a Canadian high school – I was The Foreigner (yes, with a capital f). In some strange way that I could in no way understand, I was considered responsible for the Vietnam War. I was excluded, disdained; the few friends I found did not really belong either, mainly because of their families' foreign background. School was very painful because of this exclusion. University was somewhat better: I indulged my intellectual curiosity and once again found a few friends with whom I would visit the "Foreign Students' Union", an institution at the University of Toronto where locals could go to meet foreign students.

Fleeing Canada and the anti-Americanism I had felt there became a goal that I managed to achieve – thanks to a scholarship. I came to Europe and ultimately stayed here. Unfortunately, when I arrived in Switzerland with my prized scholarship I discovered that I was very much the foreigner here. First, on the political level, the country was in the midst of a serious bout of xenophobia. The Schwarzenbach Initiative (initiated by James Schwarzenbach) was in full bloom: it aimed at limiting the number of foreigners and the length of their stay in the country. I was among the targeted: with my dark hair, olive skin and definitely un-Swiss French accent, I was seen as one of Them (again capitalised) – an unskilled Italian worker intent on invading the country and diminishing the wealth of every Swiss citizen.

A major problem for me as a foreign student in Switzerland was the completely different attitude to us foreigners. There was no Foreign Students' Union, nor was there a welcoming atmosphere of any kind. The university seemed to have cultivated a prejudice against anything foreign. My Bachelor of Arts degree from the University of Toronto, through which I had received the scholarship for studies in Switzerland, was considered by the university authorities as a *baccalauréat*. They refused categorically to believe that my B. A. degree was proof that I had completed university; that I had any more than a high school leaving certificate. I was, therefore, not allowed to attend university: from the point of view of the authorities I did not have the necessary prerequisite for university studies. I went anyway, attending some interesting lectures and writing papers for some professors who were prepared to accept me.

I was once again the outsider. Even the currency I had brought with me (my Bachelor of Arts degree) was not considered of any value in the local currency.

Two years later I was myself a Swiss citizen – through marriage with a young Swiss man. In a major effort to fit in I learned the Swiss German dialect, but remained a foreigner nonetheless.

My feeling foreign, not belonging, likely had its roots in early infancy: my mother was not able to care for the infant I was and asked her mother to take over. From an early age I felt alienated from my mother. In my inner world (of which I have not spoken in great detail in the above) there was a repeated sense of estrangement, alienation from the world around me. This also had to do with the frequent moves and with the frequent doubts of the school authorities in each new school system: were my academic accomplishments from the previous school system up to par with the new school system? Would I be allowed to continue to the next grade?

What ultimately helped me? With time I met other people who were foreigners or outsiders in society with whom I could speak openly about my feelings of alienation. But, I must say that throughout high school it was literature: I could slip into the worlds of foreign writers, participate in their worlds as an observer, not having to worry about being accepted. I could escape from my feelings of alienation and find excitement and joy in the world that I was discovering in the pages of the many books that I read about other societies.

One might wonder how it is possible for a young American girl to feel foreign in her own country of origin. I was in fact born in the United States. My parents were born in the U. S. and Canada. My grandparents had come to North America at the end of the nineteenth century. This is not something really unusual. I was a second-generation American. But, wherever I went in the U. S. and Canada I spoke with an accent different from anyone around. And then going to Canada at a time during which Americans were, to say the least, not well liked, was not as easy. Naturally I was already very sensitive to the question of not fitting in.

Add to all of this my Jewish identity, which became more problematic for me in Europe than in the United States and Canada.

As you see, I have a very personal interest in the topic of the foreigner, which I shall pursue in this book.

Organisation

I approach the topic of the foreigner from the stance of a Jungian analyst. We speak of archetypes; the term has been questioned, differentiated, rejected and remodelled again and again in many learned studies. It is an observable fact that certain motifs, *topoi*, patterns of behaviour, roles are found in practically all cultures worldwide.

One must say that the experience of these motifs is common to mankind. But the experience can have many facets – positive and negative – and various different feeling tones.

In the first chapter, "Deconstructing the Archetype of the Foreigner", I analyse the archetype of the foreigner with the help of the model constructed by Erich Neumann in his study *The Great Mother*. This is one aspect of my interest in the experience of the foreigner: being appreciated as a cook or being feared as a crook. There are many variables in the archetypal images expressing the archetype as such and I shall investigate many of them, pointing especially to the transformational processes that can take place along the lines of the opposites.

In the second chapter, entitled "The Archetypal Experience of Meeting the Foreigner and Being One in Early Cultures, Mythologies and Literary Texts", I look at the cultural complexes concerning foreigners as they presented in earlier societies through evidence based on products of the collective unconscious – from religious mythologies to fairy tales. Here we can find the basic characteristics of foreigners as seen by the respective cultures. We also get a hint of the perspective of some ancient foreigners themselves, especially Moses. This is extremely helpful for the appreciation of the other side of the phenomenon: what it is like to be a foreigner.

Naturally I find it of the utmost importance to include in this conceptual view of the foreigner the social and political implications of declaring someone a foreigner and treating him accordingly. The phenomenon of scapegoating seems to be ubiquitous. And I have discovered that the idea of monsters and their extraordinary popularity in our world today has a great deal to do with scapegoating. I call the third chapter "Monster Making/Scapegoating: One Way of Dealing with the Foreigner". In it I look more closely at the specific case of singling out and scapegoating people of Jewish descent.

In Chapter 4, "Alienation in the Modern World: Feeling Foreign", I approach the topic from the perspective of the foreigner himself, delving into modern expressions of the archetypal experience of alienation. Kafka's *Metamorphosis* shows how Gregor Samsa who felt like an outsider ultimately became one, to the point of becoming a bug who is dispensed with – rejected – by his own family. His alienation is also from his inner self. The main character represents Kafka's own inner turmoil and fears. Kafka's work is too perfectly applicable – both for terrorists and for nerds – to name two extremes faced with having to deal with their polyvalent feelings about feeling foreign, suffering from exclusion or the fear of exclusion.

Albert Camus' *L'Étranger* portrays Meursault both as an outsider in the world he lives in and a foreigner to the world of emotionality. I find *L'Étranger* so well illustrative of the absurdity of being foreign and yet being present without belonging, being a foreigner in the world of human emotions and relationships – hanging in without deep personal attachments. As for Thomas Mann's Tonio Kröger, his plight is that of all artists who cannot ever really belong to the society in which they live. The artist feels like an outsider, having rejected bourgeois society, but at the same time regrets not belonging. The underlying problem of feeling like an outsider because of one's sexual orientation Thomas Mann revealed in a slightly veiled manner in this early novella. All three of these works have been understood as largely autobiographical. Like many other modern literary works, they deal with the phenomenon of feeling foreign, meeting the foreigner within. It is called alienation.

In Chapter 5, which I entitle "The Encounter with the Foreigner in the Analytical Process", I examine, on the one hand, clients, on the other, analysts. Among my client cases some are trying to deal with their situation as foreigners in the world; others are faced with the foreign, which they encounter in themselves. The practical work in psychotherapy necessarily involves the analyst in the equation. And I propose that we analysts need to be acquainted to some extent with the experience of the foreign and also in a certain way to be foreigners in order to effectively help our clients.

References

Bair, Deirdre (2003) *Jung: A Biography*. Boston. New York and London: Little, Brown and Co.

Bauman, Zygmunt (2016) *Strangers at Our Door*. Cambridge and Malden, MA: Polity Press.

Jung, C. G. (1962) *Memories, Dreams, Reflections: An Autobiography* (trans. Richard and Clara Winston; paperback 2019). London: William Collins.

Neumann, Erich (1956) *Die grosse Mutter: der Archetyp des grossen Weiblichen*. Zurich: Rhein-Verlag.

1

DECONSTRUCTING THE ARCHETYPE OF THE FOREIGNER

Introduction: the symbolism of the foreigner

On the inner psychic level the foreigner actually represents all that is unknown; we can call it the unconscious – whatever is not in the light of consciousness, but in the shadow. The entire unconscious can actually, therefore, be called the shadow. In the self-regulating psyche, according to Jung, the process of trying to integrate these unconscious aspects is of paramount importance; it is guided by the Self. This means that the Self, the central psychic instance whose goal is individuation (the development, or better still, the unfolding of a person's potential for development) determines the way in which this process proceeds. And so, as we shall see in the final chapter on clinical work, the foreigner, the elements of the entire personality, the Self, which are yet unknown and often in some way unacceptable, are not evoked in the analytical process by force; the unfolding takes place according to the capacity of the individual to recognise, accept and integrate these unknown aspects. The Self decides the timing. This is the guiding light of Jungian work whose goal is not to provoke the client to integrate unconscious material, but rather to help the person learn to pay attention to, to care for, respect and integrate that which the individual is capable of integrating at that time. For this reason some contents may remain foreign for a long time; hypnosis, for example, is not advised to attempt to raise repressed material to consciousness by force at a time that might not be appropriate. Particularly foreign, painful or very strange or unusual contents arise at the appropriate time, when the person is capable of accepting them and not before. The Self guides the process, not the analyst, as many therapists of other schools claim. Foreign contents may remain foreign for long periods of time.

The motif of the foreigner has many dimensions. In this initial chapter my goal is to analyse the various facets of the foreigner archetype. In order to do so I shall first briefly define what I mean by the terms.

Identity: the foreigner and the non-foreigner

The term foreigner stems from the Latin *for* – meaning outside; in languages other than English the etymological root refers to the same outsiderness: *straniero* – *étranger*. According to the Duden Dictionary, *fremd* – the German word for foreign comes from Middle High German *vrem(e)de* and Old High German *fremidi* meaning distant or away (Duden 2003). He or she is an outsider, a stranger, when he comes from an other, a different country or culture; in the terms outsider or stranger the distinct otherness of the person's cultural background is not implicit. But, because of their common etymological roots I find it justifiable to use these terms interchangeably: in my experience they all indicate the phenomenon of not belonging to the local group, not sharing its identity. The analysis of the multitude of facets, or faces of the foreigner will be analysed in the following, but first to the non-foreigners.

In speaking of the foreigner, the non-foreigner is implicit, the person who belongs to the in-group, who is not from the outside and is not different. Who is the "we group" that chooses to call the others foreigners, the "them group"? How does it define itself? Although this group is not really homologous, it does claim to share to a certain consequential extent a common identity. Contemporary philosophical and socio-political discussions are very concerned with the topic of identity. Today we are witnessing a definite socio-political trend in which many countries consider themselves as a homologous group with a relatively clearly defined and fixed identity. As a result, they often tend to denigrate and even exclude those whom they call the foreigners. Demographical facts show that the supposition of sameness, of a homologous identity, is no longer and probably never was the case for most national groups. Citizens of countries always included people who themselves or whose ancestors were not originally from that country: the ancestors had been merchants, prisoners, slaves, soldiers or refugees. Migration has always been a fact of life.

However, social mobility has increased steadily since the advent of the railroad and the Industrial Revolution. More and more people at the present time are foreigners in the society in which they live. As Francis Fukuyama in his book on identity (*Identity: Contemporary Identity Politics and the Struggle for Recognition*, 2018) states, migration has become globalised. According to statistics published by the United Nations High Commissioner for Refugees, in 2018 approximately seven billion people inhabited this planet and over seven million of them were migrants.

Concerned citizens have developed nomenclatures for concepts describing the inclusion of foreigners. One very early concept was that of the "melting-pot" used to describe the way in which foreigners were to be assimilated in the United States. In 1908, the Zionist British author Israel Zangwill adopted the term for his play of that name; the 1909 production in Washington, DC very much impressed and influenced Theodore Roosevelt, the president at that time. In recent years people speak of the Canadian "mosaic", citing the example of Toronto, a city in which the ethnic groups are encouraged to keep their ethnic identities and still call themselves Canadian. The concept has also been named the "salad". Implicit is the idea that the various foreigners are not expected to assimilate, but to integrate while retaining their foreign identity as they wish.

The differentiation between assimilating, integrating and belonging is important for the phenomenology of the process of acceptance of the foreigner. The French Canadian philosopher and political scientist Charles Taylor is also particularly insistent on the moral aspect of the question of the attitude to the foreigner in society. The American philosopher Kwame Anthony Appiah, who speaks of himself as an English-Ghanaian homosexual, approaches the moral aspect of modern-day "cosmopolitanism", the need for empathy toward foreigners, as the need to "walk at least four moons in their moccasins" before judging them. The differentiation has been made between tolerance for the foreigner and respect for him or her. All of this scholarly work on the topic of the foreigner shows us how deeply the questions of the foreigner and identity have marked our world today. The mere proliferation of terms reminds us of the fact that the number of words to describe things or concepts in a language is determined by the importance of the things or concepts in that culture. The most well-known example is the numerous words for snow in the Inuit language; the Romantsch language in Switzerland has many different words for fields of grass.

The so-called postmodern man and woman may identify with and draw important aspects of their identity from the nation in which they live, in which they were born or from which their family originated. Some also identify strongly with their religion, their social group, some even with their sexual orientation or their skin colour. In this context I must briefly address the question of race. Race has long been, and still is, a category with which people identify. In the United States in the 1950s, official government forms asked people to indicate to which race they belonged. But, as Robert Wald Sussman (2016) reminds us in the introduction to his book *The Myth of Race: The Troubling Persistence of an*

Unscientific Idea, in 1950 UNESCO declared, "race is not a biological reality but a myth". As Sussman says, the concept of race is not actually scientifically valid because we all belong to the human race.

Diversity is a fact of modern life in individual countries and in individual human beings. Each of us actually has various facets, which make up our identity; composite facets. Francis Fukuyama and many others today go so far as to speak of people today having "hybrid identities".

From the point of view of Jungian psychology we think of identity as those elements of the personality with which the conscious ego identifies – the more or less conscious contents of the psyche, or, in more theoretical terms, the complexes, which a person recognises as belonging to their image of who they are, or the aspects that they identify as being part of who they are. It is possible to identify oneself, for example, as belonging to a certain religious group without this being an important part of who one feels one is or has become. I find this question especially interesting: what is it that makes a person in contemporary society say that they are a Christian, a Muslim, a Jew, a Buddhist, a Hindu? The elements that people point to as making up their identity in our world today pertain most often to nationality, profession and interests. Many would not mention their sexual orientation despite the fact that this aspect of the identity debate is very prominent in the socio-political discussion of our day and of prime importance for individuals from groups whose acceptance in society is questionable or relatively recent.

The in-group defines who is a foreigner and who is not. He or she is anyone that the in-group deems does not share the identity of the majority group.

The archetype

In Volume VIII of the *Collected Works*, Jung described archetypes as "typical modes of apprehension, and wherever we meet with uniform and regularly recurring modes of apprehension we are dealing with an archetype" (Jung, 1927: para. 280). Jung's definition of the term archetype changed throughout his lifetime, although some argue that he merely developed it in more detail throughout his life (Martin-Vallas, 2013). At any rate it has become more complex and less easily defined. Subsequent generations of Jungians have gone on to try to understand and, to a certain extent, to redefine in modern terms how they understand the term.

I shall explain here my view: the etymological meaning of the archetype is a primary, original model or pattern. Jung himself described a relatively limited number of archetypes, such as the Great Mother, The Wise Old Man, the Shadow, etc. He also described life situations that are archetypal – such as birth and death. People cannot really be archetypes, but people can and do experience typical life situations: human beings the world over and at all times know such experiences. According to Jung, the experience of humanity would be imprinted in these primary models. The best comparison is instinct. The preparedness to experience the typical situations facing human beings – a potential pattern of behaviour – would be part of the material with which an infant is born: in the same way as a child is born with arms and legs, a heart and a liver, the psychological organs would be comprised of the preparedness to act in certain situations in typically human ways. In the same way as birds build nests and then fly out when mature, so people build family structures and the young leave when mature. The idea of inborn patterns of behaviour being part of the basic chromosomal material has in most recent years been proven to be the case with many other animals, generally mammals, from dolphins to elephants to chimpanzees. Dolphins and elephants have been observed in mourning rituals. In this manner, a human child who has not known a mother or mothering would, when she later has a child, instinctively know how to act in a motherly manner. Such actions and reactions are triggered by experiences in the outside world. This has led to the idea that these patterns are emergent, as in chaos theory (Martin-Vallas, 2013). The fact that the patterns actually do emerge when triggered in the outside world, and as if along a chronological continuum, seems apparent.

Our biologically given proneness to be able to act and react in typically human ways enables us to deal with typical situations in life as they appear. This inborn proclivity to follow certain human patterns of behaviour helps us deal with life. Modern scientists often speak of us being "hard-wired" to behave in certain ways. This terminology does not correspond exactly to the archetype for several reasons. The archetype is not merely hardware: there are not only biological but also spiritual aspects in the archetype. It is more a spiritual psychosomatic whole. The archetype does not manifest just like that, but is rather a predilection for a certain type of response prompted by an experience and coloured by this and previous experiences. Structurally speaking, the archetypes constitute the central nucleus of our complexes.

Erich Neumann and the Great Mother archetype

I will go on here to discuss first Erich Neumann's model of the archetype of the Great Mother and then, using this model in an albeit less stringent manner, will analyse and deconstruct the archetype of the foreigner, as I see it.

There is naturally no human being who is a Great Mother; the archetype is rather the core of motherliness and has many different and contrasting facets, and is expressed in many different symbolic images. The powerful, energy laden, even numinous experience of the Great Mother is constellated whenever one of the facets is met in the course of life. Neumann defined the central, what he calls the "elementary", trait of the Great Mother, as containing. This means that all aspects of motherliness are basically about the phenomenon of being a container – physically and spiritually containing the other. Neumann went on to differentiate the transformative processes, which can take place within the sphere of motherliness – on encountering the Great Mother. The Great Mother is the "archetype as such". Anthony Stevens, in *Archetype Revisited* (2015: 284), defines it as an "innate neuropsychic potential … actualized in the form of archetypal images, motifs, ideas, relationships and behaviours". The archetype as such exists *in potentia* and becomes manifest in various different archetypal images. Neumann distinguished both positive and negative developments evoked by encounters with figures embodying aspects of the Great Mother – from development to death, from inspiration to madness. He also named mythological figures, which he felt embody these various aspects.

The archetype of the foreigner

I will approach the archetype of the foreigner in a similar manner to Neumann (see Figure 1.1). More detailed descriptions of the individual archetypal images will be presented in the following chapter, which goes into a more in-depth treatment of mythological texts from the collective unconscious.

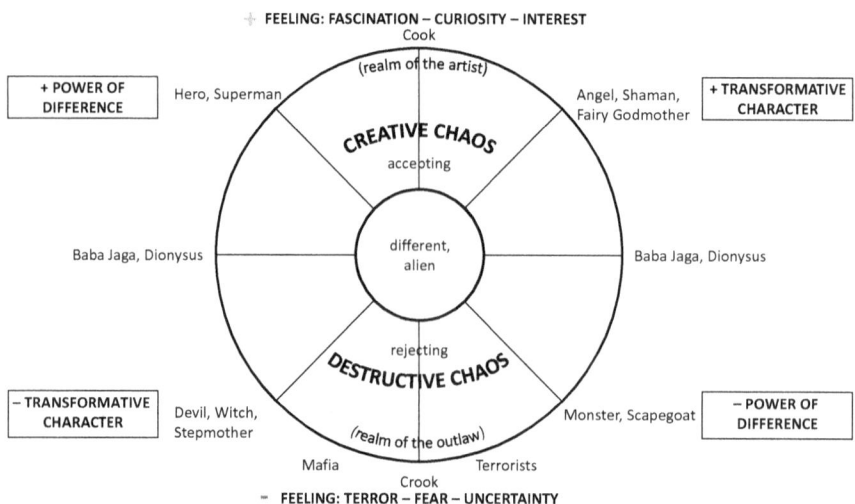

FIGURE 1.1 The archetype of the foreigner
Source: Neumann (1956: 80)

The elementary character of the foreigner and the basic attitudes

The elementary character of the foreigner is his differentness, his alienness. He is not like the others, he is different. Around the circle we must think of gradations. All of the manifestations and reactions to the foreigner are on a spectrum leading from one extreme to the other. The top half of the circle I call the acceptance of the foreigner, allowing his differentness to be accepted, respected and more or less integrated. This is the domain of creative chaos, which can lead to a new order. The predominant feeling tone here would spread from interest, to attraction, to curiosity, even to fascination. Among the gradations on the interest side we find extreme interest, in the sense of exoticism; this can be tinged with a lack of respect toward the foreigner as a human being. We know this attitude, for example, in the way in which up until the middle of the twentieth century members of African tribes were put on display in zoological gardens and even world fairs. This kind of colonialist attitude did not take into consideration the fact that foreigners are human beings who have feelings. But exoticism has also manifested in less disrespectful manners, for example in the *chinoiserie* of the eighteenth and the *japonisme* of the nineteenth century. The interest then was mainly aesthetic and led Westerners to collect and be inspired by objects from China and Japan. Albeit they sometimes purchased these objects without paying fair prices, i.e. paying proper respect to the owners. Thus, in some way, in exoticism the foreigner is less respected, less accepted as equal.

The bottom half of the circle is that of rejection, where the encounter is tinged with negative feelings – uncomfortable feelings of uncertainty, fear, even terror. This side is the domain of chaos, which tends to be destructive. The foreigner in this area is rather seen as a danger, even an outlaw who is to be avoided, rejected, excluded, even to be exterminated, as in the case of the scapegoat.

The cook versus the crook

At the top of the circle I have placed the positive developments of acceptance that can lead to appreciation of the foreigner as a creative power. He can inspire and enrich the collective or the individual who encounters him. I call this pole the cook; the cook represents all the possible creative aspects of the foreigner who contributes something to the society, which it considers valuable. In our world today the most obviously widely appreciated foreigners can be seen as the exotic cooks who bring recipes and culinary tradition and knowledge from their country of origin to a relatively large number of members of the new society. I have chosen the term cook as a catchall term for any creative individual who contributes to the foreign society; it is also the domain of the artist. We know many examples of musicians, dancers, writers, painters, even exceptionally creative businessmen who, having left their country of origin, bring new and very much appreciated talents to the new society. The in-group appreciates their contributions; they are integrated, albeit partially, because they are still, and may always remain, identified as foreigners. This leads me to an interesting question to which I have no definitive answer. One would have to do some serious international research on this question, perhaps with a questionnaire presented to such foreigners, asking them the extent to which these cooks/artists continue to feel like foreigners in the new society. And, if they do continue to feel like foreigners, to what extent do they feel this identity to be offensive and hurtful, or to what extent do they like being identified as foreigners?

At the other, opposite end of the pole are the negative developments that have to do with the rejection of the foreigner. We know too well how xenophobic political powers often describe the foreigner as a criminal force, seeking to destroy or steal from the in-group. This is the crook side of the spectrum. This polarity "the cook versus the crook" knows many intermediate shades and many diverse images, from the artist as we have seen above to the outlaw – a rascal, a thief, a member of the Mafia, a rapist, a terrorist.

Again and again we see how in transformative processes the archetype can flip from one side to the other. The cook can become the crook, the crook a cook. This is also apparent in the following archetypal images.

The power of the hero and the monster

Now, back to the upper side of the circle and the positive aspects and the feasible transformative processes that can take place here. The hero foreigner, embodied, for example, in Superman is, like the cook, the good foreigner. The power of difference, which he represents, is sometimes attributed to foreigners in a negative manner (the opposite side of the circle). They can be seen as powerful freaks or monsters. Bent on the destruction of the new society, they become the scapegoats who must be eliminated. We know how easily the singled-out minority can become the enemy, the monster, the scapegoat, as we shall see in more detail in Chapter 3. Suffice it to note here the attribution of great intelligence, wealth and power to Jewish people – philo-Semitism – can and does flip to the opposite and become anti-Semitism.

Liminal figures

There are also figures that stand on the boundary between these two poles – liminal figures; whether they can, on being included in the society, bring a creative addition to the society or, on being rejected, become destructive, depends on how they are welcomed. The figure of the Baba Jaga in Russian fairy tales well exemplifies this polarity. Can she become a positive transformative power? Or will she destroy the person who meets her. In the next chapter we shall pursue this question.

The foreigner and the spiritual

The most impressive positive foreigner on the spiritual side is the angel of the Bible who brings about a positive transformational process in bringing new life to Abraham and Leah. His opposite is the devil, also a spiritual figure, who in fairy tales is often disguised as a stranger, a foreign beggar. He brings destruction through, for example, bargaining for the souls of those he meets. Along with the devil we frequently find the witch or the evil stepmother; they are foreigners, the latter because she does not belong to the family. But, in fact, as we have seen in the previous chapter, their negative transformative powers ultimately lead to positive transformations. They themselves are not transformed, but are generally killed.

The foreign god Dionysus, god of wine can bring about madness (in his maenads, for example) through inebriation or he can be the cause of inspiration. In this way he can also be considered a liminal figure. But, at the same time he must be placed alongside these spiritual outsiders. The shaman, too, often chosen by the society because of some unusual, psychic gifts, is often a person who in some way is different from the other, normal tribe members.

The anthropologist Max Gluckman, in his *Politics, Law and Ritual in Tribal Society* (originally published in 1965) was engaged in field studies on the special position of foreigners, strangers – all of those people who did not belong to the specific social system in tribal societies. On the one hand he pointed out, these foreigners can be "called in to solve internal crises in the life of the group" (Gluckman, 1982: 101), and be asked to play the role of mediators. On the other hand, he also observed foreigners who were seen not only as shamans but as prophets with supernatural powers. Gluckman compared these specific roles of outsiders in tribal societies to those of the court jesters in the royal courts of Europe. The fool whose foreignness allows him to see things differently and to express this difference is, in this way, similar to the cook. His freedom seems to have been more pronounced. Is this the category we analysts belong to? I shall pursue this question in the final chapter.

The victim or the persecutor

There is also another facet of the foreigner to whom I have not attributed a place in the diagram: he is neither cook nor crook, and is just trying to find his way as a foreigner in a foreign land. He or she – as for example a refugee – can seem to be a victim; a poor, underprivileged, person, ignorant of the tools necessary for integration into society and lacking knowledge of the language and the customs. He can find himself at various places in the spectrum, tending toward either end. He can find himself somewhere in the middle ground, just a foreigner who is more or less integrated in the new society. In fairy tales he can be the poor beggar who can, on being treated well, be helpful. He can take a place in the realm of the artist (the cook). But, sometimes the victim can over-identify with this role and, as we know, extreme one-sidedness can turn into its opposite. The victim can, feeling rejected, turn into a perpetrator or a crook who takes revenge on society. This seems to be one of the dynamics involved in a great number of terrorist attacks in recent times. I shall be examining this phenomenon in Chapter 4 which deals with alienation.

The perspective of the foreigner

An important aspect of the archetypal experience, the perspective of a woman who is a mother, was not the focus of interest for Neumann. His view is objective – what it is like to meet up with, encounter, to be faced with a manifestation of the archetype. He was not interested in the question of what it is like to be a mother, what it is like to live the archetypal experience of being a mother. The encounter with the foreigner is, without doubt, a typical human experience; but one can also, and everyone has to a certain extent, known the experience of being a foreigner, be it as a world traveller, a cosmopolite or even as a new child in a school or a new kid on the block. This aspect of the foreigner is also of great interest for our discussion and especially in the context of psychotherapy.

On the positive side of the spectrum we can find real interest, a sense of curiosity for the new culture, which is foreign to the foreigner. A striving for inclusion, for appreciation and not denigration can lead to extraordinary ambition, as we often see in families of immigrants. The repercussions on their descendants are often anything but helpful for the latter's development, but create a serious and sometimes very damaging source of stress.

The negative pole of the experience is insecurity, feeling excluded or rejected hurts. How to deal with the rejection? This insecurity can lead to various reactions – to a depressive state or to an aggressive one. Among my foreign clientele, prejudices abound about the in-group that does not recognise, value or accept them. Various degrees of aggression accompany these value judgements. And, of course, this attitude has many different manifestations, the most extreme of which I shall be discussing in detail in a later chapter – that of the outsider, bullied or otherwise undervalued, excluded foreigner who lashes out at society physically and terrorises the local population. Here the example of terrorists – be they Salafists, Isis fighters or outsiders from within the society (social rejects or deeply disturbed individuals like Anders Breivik who, in 2011, attacked and killed 77 innocent – mostly young – people on a vacation island in Norway because of his hatred of multiculturalism) – lies at the most extreme pole of this development.

An anecdote from my practice

Before I go on to discuss the archetypal needs of the foreigner I would like to relate a brief illustrative anecdote from my practice.

I once worked with a man whose German family moved to the US when he was a little boy. His sense of insecurity in the new country whose language and culture were foreign to him was obvious. In the world outside he felt rather helpless; he could have readily identified himself as a foreigner victim. But, he watched lots of television. The movies he saw about the Nazi period offered him the possibility of identifying with strong and powerful German men – quite the contrast to his experiences at school and in his new American neighbourhood. So, one day, as his family was entertaining company, he burst into the room with the proud proclamation, loud and clear, "I am a Nazi!". His family was accordingly shocked, as were the visitors. But how was this little boy to know that being a Nazi meant anything other than being strong and powerful? It seemed to offer the perfect solution for his terrible feelings of insecurity and weakness in this new and foreign culture called America!

Archetypal human needs

Absolutely essential in considering the psychology and the situation of the foreigner himself is the question of the archetypal needs of human beings. The need to be recognised and valued is second to the top of Abraham

Maslow's pyramid of human needs (Maslow, 1943): he calls it esteem. Francis Fukuyama calls it the need for recognition (Fukuyama, 2018: 35). Very closely related is the need at the top of Maslow's pyramid, the need for self-actualisation, feeling one can achieve one's full potential. But, again, Maslow places in third place the need for love/belonging. I, too, believe it is a basic need to feel embedded and appreciated by the society in which one lives. As we have seen in the deconstructed archetype, this goal (becoming the cook) is not always achieved. The exclusion and even rejection of the foreigner is daily life for large numbers of people in society. Its repercussions are serious deterrents to a peaceful life in society today. In the following chapters I shall be looking at terrorists as perpetrators whose exclusion has favoured if not caused their destructive developments.

In the following chapter on foreigners in mythological texts I shall be looking in detail at Moses as a foreigner whose lack of basic archetypal needs led to his becoming the leader of the Hebrew people.

References

Duden. 2003. *Deutsches Universalwörterbuch* (5th edition). Mannheim, Leipzig, Wien, and Zurich: Duden Verlag.

Fukuyama, Francis (2018) *Identity: Contemporary Identity Politics and the Struggle for Recognition*. Great Britain: Farrar, Straus and Giroux.

Gluckman, Max (1982) *Politics, Law and Ritual in Tribal Society*. Oxford: Basil Blackwell.

Jung, C. G. (1927) 'Instinct and the Unconscious'. *The Collected Works, Vol. VIII* (English Edition). Princeton, NJ: Princeton University Press.

Martin-Vallas, Francois (2013) 'Are Archetypes Transmitted or Emergent? A Response to Christian Roesler' (translated from the French by Ann Kutek), *The Journal of Analytical Psychology*, 58: 278–285.

Maslow, Abraham (1943) 'A Theory of Human Motivation', *Psychological Review*, 50(4): 370–390.

Neumann, Erich (1956) *Die grosse Mutter: der Archetyp des grossen Weiblichen*. Zurich: Rhein-Verlag.

Stevens, Anthony (2015) *Archetype Revisited: An Updated Natural History of the Self*. Hove and New York: Routledge.

Sussman, Robert W. (2016) *The Myth of Race: The Troubling Persistence of an Unscientific Idea* (4th edn). London: Harvard University Press.

Zangwill, Israel (1908 [2015]) *The Melting-Pot*. USA/Poland: Jefferson Publication.

2

THE ARCHETYPAL EXPERIENCE OF MEETING THE FOREIGNER AND BEING ONE IN EARLY CULTURES, MYTHOLOGIES AND LITERARY TEXTS

The prominence of the topic

One of the fascinating aspects surrounding the topic of the foreigner is the prominence of the topic in so many religious texts, which, for the sake of clarity, I shall designate as mythologies. Early Sanskrit texts refer to foreigners as *mleccha* (which means something like bla-bla-bla), an abject people incapable of speaking correct Sanskrit. Ancient Hindu texts restrict the welcoming of foreigners to the caste; in contrast, Buddhism insists on the importance of welcoming and feeding the stranger, regardless of caste. In ancient Egypt, the attitude to foreigners went through many different phases, but the basic assumption was that Egyptian order was the divine order (*maat*). Foreigners who lived among the Egyptians, even slaves, who complied with Egyptian laws were accepted. Those who did not comply or who lived outside Egypt represented chaos or (*isfet*) and were to be conquered and then integrated into the kingdom.

In ancient Greece, foreigners were called *metics*, from the word *métoikos* (a word meaning to change dwelling). Although they were accepted within the city, they were obliged to pay a special tax and were not allowed to own property or to vote. Foreigners from Doric areas were not as well accepted as those of Ionian origin. And, as the people of Platea had helped Athens in war, they enjoyed a special position among the foreigners.

The case of Dionysus is most interesting: he was considered of foreign origin as he was born in Thrace and subsequently travelled to India and Egypt before finally arriving in Greece. He was, therefore, considered the god of the foreigners and was meant to protect them. Through his hermaphrodite being, his identity as the god of wine and his association with the ecstasy but also the madness that wine can provoke, he is a god of border zones – a liminal deity. He represented the world of divine madness – the chaotic. The secret Dionysian Mysteries involved a descent into the underworld and a return to life, as is fitting for the encounter with chaos. The wildness of his followers, the maenads, also belongs to the world of chaos and not to the orderly world of civilisation.

Ultimately, as mentioned in the previous chapter, in most early cultures and even today in xenophobic societies, the foreigner, because he does not fit in with the local culture, represents chaos. Chaos must be kept outside of the borders of the prevailing cultural order. This is the predominant opinion in xenophobic societies, or, more precisely, in societies during a xenophobic phase. That this should have been the case in earlier times is, to a certain extent, understandable: danger was imminent on meeting someone who did not belong. One could not know his intentions and needed to be aware of potential danger, be prepared to fight to protect what one considered as one's own property, children, women, land. The insecure citizen today seems, however, also to need to feel encompassed within the borders of the prevailing social order and therefore feel protected from whatever he judges as not belonging. Trespassing is dangerous. Such hegemonic cultural attitudes are meant to provide security by guaranteeing the power of the reigning social order and its representatives. As we have seen, contemporary philosophers and social psychologists are recently concerned with the morality of such attitudes, which neither reflect nor respect the diversity of present-day societies; they have adopted other images to describe modern-day cosmopolitan societies. In fact, contemporary people and societies have a multitude of dimensions, which define their identity. It is the relatively recent renewal of the tendency to nationalism, which attempts to limit and define the dominant local culture. It alone is to prevail, to rule: all are meant to adapt, to comply. In early, collective societies this rule was unquestioned.

The Hebrew Bible

With the advent of monotheism there appears a more consistently welcoming approach to the phenomenon of the foreigner. The most spectacular example is to be found in the myth of Avram and Sarai, the couple from whom the entire Hebrew nation supposedly stems. Their story is so impressive as to have been adopted with few revisions by Muslim and Christian mythologies. Avram and Sarai themselves knew the experience of being foreigners as they had been commanded by God to travel from their home to several different countries. Nothing is known of their interaction with the natives: the Bible does not portray explicitly the inner life of its personae. But, the fact that they had been foreigners does, I believe, determine their approach to the foreigners who arrive on their doorstep in the text in question here. Three strangers (foreigners) arrive and Avram commands a meal for them, offering them unadulterated hospitality, what Jacques Derrida would call "unconditional hospitality" (Kakoloris, 2015). That these three men were angels was not apparent; only later does one learn that this was the case. They leave saying that Sarai will have a child who will be the founder of a multitude that will believe in the one God. Sarai, who is supposedly 89 years old at the time, laughs and one year later Isaac (whose name means laugh) is born (Genesis 18).

The continuation of the story is less important in the context of the topic of foreigner. However, Avram's reaction to God's demand of the sacrifice of Jacob reveals one major way in which the new religion is different and foreign. Avram came from a culture in which it was not unusual for children to be sacrificed. It was entirely within his ken to sacrifice his child to a deity. But, this deity proves to be different: he rejects the sacrifice and makes only one demand: Avram must promise that he and his descendants will pay allegiance to and obey him as the people of the covenant. This change of paradigm is the crucial moment of the new religion.

1. And when Avram was ninety years old and nine, the LORD appeared to Avram, and said unto him, I am the Almighty God; walk before me, and be thou perfect.
2. And I will make my covenant between me and thee, and will multiply thee exceedingly.
3. And Avram fell on his face: and God talked with him, saying,
4. As for me, behold, my covenant is with thee, and thou shalt be a father of many nations.
5. Neither shall thy name any more be called Avram, but thy name shall be Avraham; for a father of many nations have I made thee.

(Genesis 17: 1–5)

The founding mother and father of the people of the covenant are given new names: Avram becomes Avraham and Sarai, Sarah: the deity shows his power by giving them names, granting them a new identity.

In the Hebrew Bible there are countless stories of inhospitable towns whose population is destroyed, because they did not welcome foreigners in the same generous manner as Avram. The best-known example is that of Sodom and Gomorrah; a less known story is that of Gibeah in Benjamin, not far from Jerusalem. There the locals abused and killed the concubine of a visiting foreigner; as a consequence, practically the entire population is wiped out, with the consent of God (Judges 20).

The Hebrew Bible constantly invokes the acceptance of the foreigner: after all, the Hebrew people itself was constantly in the position of the foreigner, wandering from land to land until they were to reach their Holy Land, promised by their God, their "land of milk and honey".

> And if a stranger sojourns with thee in your land, ye shall not vex him. But the stranger that dwelleth with you shall be unto you as one born, among you, and thou shalt love him as thyself; for ye were strangers in the land of Egypt: I *am* the Lord your God.
>
> *(Leviticus 19:33–34)*

and

> Thou shalt neither vex a stranger nor oppress him: for ye were strangers in the land of Egypt.
>
> *(Exodus 22:21)*

Another facet of the foreigner question in this mythology is the story of Moses who, as he was rescued as a baby by the pharaoh's daughter, lived as a foreigner in Egypt. Although the Bible does not really get into psychological questions, if we read between the lines we do discover an emotional state in the case of Moses. He names his first child Gershom (the Hebrew word *ger* means sojourner) and he explains this by saying, "I have been a stranger in a strange land" (Exodus 2:22). This brief comment tells us that the experience of being a foreigner marked this man. One of the basic archetypal needs not so easily or readily attained by the foreigner was missing for Moses – the feeling of belonging. Other needs that we have seen in the first chapter can be frustrated for more or less long periods of time: the need for a sense of being appreciated by society (the lack of which leads to a lack in self-esteem) and a lack in a perspective for future development. Without a sense of hope for the future, the foreigner can feel powerless and lack a sense of meaning in life. How he manages to deal with this frustration is a major and even urgent question for society.

In the case of Moses, his anger at this frustration seems to get the better of him. On seeing a slave driver beat a Hebrew slave, Moses kills the slave driver and flees from Egypt. It looks as if he must have realised for some reason not explained by the Bible that the Hebrew slaves were his "brethren" (Exodus 2:11). Moses felt empathy for the slave – the empathy, which scientists today describe as most especially directed toward people we are familiar with. Or did he perhaps also feel the compulsion to do something monumental for this people to whom he wanted to belong? Did he need to redeem himself from his survivor's guilt of having been saved from the death of all other male Hebrew infants, of having been brought up in the pharaoh's palace? These are questions to which we have no answers. At any rate, Moses is courageous and adventurous and takes on the task of leading the people out of Egypt. But, he is also full of anger toward the people who are impatient and not as appreciative as he would have hoped. They complain, for example, in an important passage about the lack of water during their 40-year wanderings. Moses is commanded by God to speak to the rock so that it will give water. Instead he smites the rock. This act of disobedience leads to Moses' death before being able to enter the promised land.

It is not by chance that this man, brought up as a foreigner in Egypt and also a foreigner in his native land, is chosen to lead the people out of Egyptian captivity to the promised land. As we shall see, many stories of mythological proportions (including fairy tales) portray the foreigner as the only one capable of facing the difficult situation and solving the problems threatening the local civilisation.

The Christian Bible

The New Testament also encourages hospitality to strangers, referring directly back to the encounter of Avram and Sarai with the angels. "Be not forgetful to entertain strangers: for thereby some have entertained angels unawares" (Hebrews 13:2).

This attitude is basic to the narrative of the Christian faith which goes so far as to express the hope and/or belief that when the people believe in Jesus foreignness will cease to exist. "Where there is neither Greek nor Jew, circumcision nor uncircumcision, Barbarian, Scythian, bonds *nor* free: but Christ *is* all, and in all" (Colossians 3:11) and, in a similar tone, "Now ye are no more strangers and foreigners, but said fellow citizens with the saints, and of the household of God" (Ephesians 3:19). Hospitality is a basic tenet mentioned explicitly in many texts including Romans, which states, people are to be "given to hospitality" (Romans 12:13). Jesus himself, according to his apostles, identified with the stranger or the foreigner. His meeting with the Samaritan woman at the well is a good example (St. John 4). Even initially, Jesus is the foreigner who attracts foreigners and later cares for them. In the Gospel according to

Matthew, "For I was hungred, and ye gave me meat: I was thirsty. And ye gave me drink: I was a stranger and ye took me in" (Matthew 25:35). The story of the baby Jesus begins with the rejection of Mary and Joseph, seen as strangers who, having left their home in Nazareth, sought shelter in Bethlehem, but were denied this shelter. They were foreigners in Bethlehem; this initial situation of homelessness is basic to the story of Jesus as the saviour of humanity. The four wise men – foreigners from the East – come with exotic gifts to welcome and rejoice in the wondrous birth of the baby in a stall in Bethlehem. The narrative of the Jesus figure who becomes the Christ (Messiah) continues with repeated encounters with outsiders, people who have been excluded or rejected, such as Maria Magdalena. The saviour figure accepts and protects them all. Ultimately, he is rejected by the reigning religious authorities because of his new and different approach: he is crucified by the reigning political powers because he represents a foreign cult, which seems to be causing too much disturbance in the Roman Empire.

Muslim teachings

Ishmael, a prophet and direct ancestor of Mohammed, was sent out into the desert with his mother, the slave woman Hagar, by his father Avram because of his wife, Sarai's jealousy. Mohammed himself in his journey from Mecca to Medina lived the experience of a foreigner. The Muslim religion accordingly shows great care and respect of the foreigner. In the Quran the stranger is called "Ibn Al-Sabil" (wayfarer, traveller or sojourner). The recent German translation is most impressive: "*Sohn des Weges*/my translation: son of the way/path" (Bobzin, 2010/2019: 154). Even if the Ibn Al-Sabil happens to be wealthy, the devout Muslim is obliged to give him money. The spoils of war are also to be shared with him.

> And know that whatever spoils you gain, to God belongs its fifth, and to the Messenger, and the relatives, and the orphans, and the poor, and to the wayfarer, provided you believe in God and in what We revealed to Our servant on the Day of Distinction, the day when the two armies met. God is Capable of everything.
>
> *(Quran 8:41)*

Charity is for "the parents, and the relatives, and the orphans, and the poor, and the wayfarer" (Quran 2:215). Similarly, in chapter nine, called "Repentance", charity is to be given to "the traveller in need" (Quran 9:60). Chapter 30 includes among those to whom one is to "give his rights" "the destitute, and the wayfarer" (Quran 30:38).

do good to parents,
> kinsfolk, orphans, Al-Masdkin (the poor), the
> neighbour who is near of kin, the neighbour
> who is a stranger, the companion by your
> side, the wayfarer (you meet), and those
> (slaves) whom your right hands possess.

(Quran 30:38)

Chapter 59 goes so far as to refer to refugees as the sincere:

> To the poor refugees who were driven out of their homes and
> their possessions, as they sought the favor of God and His approval,
> and came to the aid of God and His Messenger. These are the
> sincere.

(Quran: 59:8)

But, a person who gives water to pilgrims is not considered as holy as
a believer:

> Do you consider giving water to pilgrims and maintaining the
> Sacred Mosque the same as believing in God and the Last Days and
> striving in God's path? They are not equal in God's sight. God
> does not guide the unjust people.

(Quran 9:19)

In Sunan Abu Dawud's hadith, *The Book of Etiquette*, the comforts of the
traveller are to be taken into consideration: anyone who cuts down
a tree under which travellers seek shade will be destroyed by Allah who
will "put his head in the Fire" (Abu Dawud, 2014: 474).

Traditionally in Muslim culture the foreigner is called a *"dhimmi"* and
has certain established rights and obligations. The *dhimmi* must pay a tax,
a so-called head tax (which, by the way, was often demanded of Jewish
populations instead of eliminating them) to the local Muslim government, but is allowed freedom to practise his/her religion, even to be
subject to his own religion's court of law. This would mean that these
societies were a kind of mosaic at a very early time. The same is true of
the Hebrew societies as described in the Bible. Many Muslim states no
longer observe this ruling. In general, modern states do not demand
taxes of foreigners; nor do they allow them to be ruled by their own
religious courts of law. In Germany, for example, there are often political
discussions when certain religious minorities attempt to apply their own
codes of values and laws to the members of their religion living in

Germany. Compliance with the *"Leitkultur"*, which means the dominant culture of the political state in which the people reside, is required from the members of a foreign culture residing in modern political states.

Fairy tales

Fairytales, like mythologies, as products of the collective unconscious, also provide interesting information about the respective culture's attitude to the foreigner. In Grimms' fairy tales, as Catherine Crowther, Jane Haynes and Kathleen Newton pointed out in their article on fairy tales in *Contemporary Jungian Analysis* (1998), the Grimm brothers (who collected and also amended folk tales at the beginning of the nineteenth century in Germany) were long thought to have collected tales from the oral tradition. In fact, they also took tales from Perrault's collection. And, as they were intent on presenting a certain image of German and European culture, they made important amendments, inclusions and exclusions, which suited this image.

In fairytales, as generally in the Bible, the inner lives of the characters are not described in great detail. The characters do not show any special interest in the foreigners they meet up with, neither where they came from, nor what exactly caused their transformation – e.g. their suddenly being transformed into an animal. The only thing that interests the characters is their actions within the setting of the tale. The initial meeting with the foreigner usually signals an imminent potential danger, threatening the life of the hero/heroine. In this category one must place not only the hungry wolves and the devils posing as poor beggars but also the stepmothers; the latter, new in the family, an exogamous member of the familial group, are therefore also foreigners. Their role never seems to be positive – on the surface.

On a deeper psychological level, however, accepting and even welcoming the foreigner is most often an important element ultimately leading to the positive development of the central character. I am thinking, for example of "The Maiden without Hands". When her father meets a stranger who happens to be the devil the deal he makes with the devil leads to the girl's leaving home with no hands. But ultimately, she is not only saved by a prince; she also has a child, gets new real hands and lives happily ever after as a queen. Sleeping Beauty, rejected by her stepmother, is welcomed by the seven dwarves with whom she lives. When she seems to have died from eating the poisoned apple, she once again is found, revived and married by the foreign prince. Without Cinderella's evil stepmother, the girl would never have met the fairy godmother or the prince. Interesting, however, is the fact that at the end of such stories the evil stepmother devil is usually punished, and the devil is tricked. The stepmother is not integrated, but her encounter and learning to deal with her – as a representative of the shadow – fosters development and leads to a new and positive development: the heroine becomes capable of developing her potential.

In all of these examples, and others, the encounter with the foreigner as a shadow figure is guided by the Self with the goal of fostering the development of the personality. This in no way means that the encounter feels positive – it can be very cruel and painful – but it does encourage the ultimate unfolding of the personality. The moral of such stories: one may meet up with many hardships in life, but if you are good and helpful, modestly accepting your fate and believe in God, things will turn out well.

Obviously, the figure of the fairy godmother, who so frequently appears on the scene, is also a foreigner. She is the good foreigner who magically makes things all better. In Russian fairy tales we come upon the figure of Baba Jaga; she is especially interesting in this context of the encounter with the foreigner. This witch is essentially either positive or negative depending on the way in which one reacts when meeting her. If one welcomes her, she acts like a good fairy. Otherwise she can be very cruel. But as we have seen above, in practically all fairy tales the encounter with the apparently evil stranger turns out to be the catalyst for future positive development, allowing the stasis of a difficult life situation to be transformed into a more fruitful, fuller life.

There is one extraordinary exception to the portrayal of the foreigner as a catalyst for a positive development in Grimms' fairy tales: the portrayal of the character invariably called "the Jew". Several tales ("The Jew in the Brambles", "The Jewry Stone" and "The Good Bargain") feature a man, described merely as "a Jew", usually unkempt and money-hungry who cheats and/or kills an innocent person. At the end of the tale he is punished by death. He represents true evil and is and remains the evil foreigner; he has no transformative power and is never redeemed but is and remains eternally evil. This cultural complex surrounding the Jewish population is based on the scapegoat mentality of the culture, which singled out the largest minority among them as responsible for all evils in their world.

The foreigner as a religious leader

Invariably religious leaders identify themselves as different, somehow foreign. As bringers of new truths, new customs, new laws and morals, they naturally are all basically rejecting the old traditional order. They need to be foreign. But, it is not only the fact of their identifying as foreigners with a foreign or strange new message, nor their generosity in encounters

with foreigners that is common in the mythologies of these three mono-
theistic religions. The founder of the religion always undertakes a voyage
and physically knows the archetypal experience of foreignness, of being
foreign in a new society and becoming the object of the local people's
attention as a foreigner. This is also true of the Buddha whom I have
not mentioned before; he is said to have travelled to preach to Eastern
India and Sri Lanka. The voyage undertaken by the new religious leader
is often wandering physically over land or water. These voyages are, on
the one hand, a practical necessity in pre-internet times. The leader and
his followers must spread the word of the new religion in order to persuade and recruit more and more followers. But, at times, the voyage is
rather an imaginative excursion into a new land in the sense of a spiritual
journey, a night-sea journey. Voyages are always part of a developmental
process, the discovery and implementation of newness, new ideas and
new beliefs. This, too, is an archetypal pattern found throughout time in
the most varied of cultures. And, thus, necessarily, the questions surrounding foreignness, being a foreigner and being treated like a foreigner
necessarily shaped the message of the founding fathers of these religions.

The foreigner as an adventurer

Looking back to Antiquity we have found the motif of the voyage
occupying a prominent place in the culture; the frequent voyage here
also always implies encountering the foreign and also being the foreigner, taking risks in approaching the foreign and also acquiring
something new through the contact with the exotic but also poten-
tially dangerous land and its population. From Homer's *Odyssey* to
Jack Kerouak's *On the Road*, the voyage, and the encounter with the
foreigner, the experience of being foreign are central. Many of the
most famous literary works of all times have been devoted to the central topic of the voyage – from *Beowulf* (975–1010) to Cervantes' *Don
Quixote* (1605 + 1615), from Dante's *Inferno* (1320) to *Canterbury Tales*
(around 1400) to Bunyan's *Pilgrim's Progress* (1678). The topic has
obviously fascinated mankind for centuries. But, the way in which the
traveller experiences these voyages – the subjective point of view – is
seldom a topic of direct and detailed observation.

  The motif of the voyage also plays a prominent role in Western literature as of the eighteenth century – from Voltaire to Jonathan Swift. But
here again the perspective is not internal. We do not discover a great
deal about how the foreigner feels in the new and foreign environment.
The author's interest is more directed to the observation, the satirical
observation of his own society masked as criticism of the foreign land.

The most we discover, for example, about Samuel Gulliver's reactions to being tied up by the Lilliputians is a feeling of amusement. No deeper feelings are revealed. This is not what Swift was interested in portraying.

In the nineteenth century, tales of adventure, such as Jules Verne's *Twenty-thousand Leagues under the Sea* and Lewis Carol's *Alice in Wonderland*, describe the experiences of the narrator or the main figure as a foreigner or an outsider in an exotic world. The authors take great pains to describe in detail these fascinating worlds under the sea or beyond the looking glass. Only to a very limited extent do they delve into the inner world of their characters, the way they experienced the foreign or felt foreign.

The twentieth century takes a different turn: literary texts become focused less on the outward voyage, but rather on the question of feeling foreign in the sense of feeling alienated from society (often one's own) or from oneself. At the beginning of the twentieth century we find texts on alienation in the sense of deep and perturbing alienation from oneself (Kafka), from society (Thomas Mann) and even from the human condition (Albert Camus). This change in perspective is, of course, of great interest for us here. It is the subject of the following chapter on alienation.

References

Abu Dawud, Sunan (2014) *The Book of Etiquette*. Available from: https://archive.org./details/SunanAbuDawudVol.111160EnglishArabic

Bobzin, Hartmut (2010, 2019) *Der Koran: Aus Dem Arabischen Neu Übertragen Von Hartmut Bobzin Unter Mitarbeit Von Katharina Bobzin*. Munich: Verlag C. H. Beck.

Crowther, Catherine, Haynes, Jane, and Newton, Kathleen (1998) 'Myth and Fairy Tales: The Psychological Use of Fairy Tales'. In *Contemporary Jungian Analysis: Post-Jungian Perspectives from the Society of Analytical Psychology*, eds. Ian Alister and Christopher Hauke, (pp. 211–228). London and New York: Routledge.

Grimm's *Märchen*. Erlangen: Karl Müller.

Itani, Talal A. trans. (2012) *The Quran*. Modern English translation. Dallas and Beirut: ClearQuran.

Kakoloris, Gerasimos (2015) 'Derrida and the Ethics of Hospitality'. In *The Ethics of Subjectivity: Perspectives since the Dawn of Modernity*, ed. Elvis Imafidon (pp. 144–156). New York: Palgrave Macmillan.

The Holy Bible. Authorized or King James Version. New York: Thomas Nelson & Sons.

3

MONSTER MAKING/SCAPEGOATING

One way of dealing with the foreigner

Introduction

I began being interested in monsters while working on the question of foreigners and how they have been treated in society from earlier times until today. I have come to realise that monsters can be very diverse creatures, but they all have a few characteristics in common, the most obvious of which is that they are invariably foreign and frightening.

In the following I will define the concept of monster and how it has been understood in different cultures; then I shall go on to examine the significance of the fact that human beings from time immemorial seem to have created monsters; symbolising fear of the foreign, they are too frequently projected onto foreigners themselves.

Wherefore monsters?

There are two possible etymological roots for the word monster. It can come from the Latin *monstrare* meaning to show or, more likely, from the Latin *monere* which means to warn. The prevalence of magical thinking in earlier times when scientific knowledge and scientific explanations were lacking makes sense for us. The unexpected and inexplicable occurrence – the appearance of the abnormal, the freakish – either a lack of rain, the birth of a deformed child, the prevalence of sudden deaths from an unknown illness with strange symptoms – all of these unusual occurrences must have been frightening and were considered signs of, or warnings of imminent danger. There is a beautiful, poetic example of this mentality in Shakespeare's *Julius Caesar* (Thorndike, 1973) in which Casca (in Act I, scene iii), fearing Caesar's ambitiousness when he returns victorious to Rome, reports of strange things that he has seen and heard. He begins by asking Cicero, "Are you not moved when all the sway of earth Shakes like a thing unfirm?" And he goes on to describe the especially frightening natural phenomena that he has been witness to just now: "a tempest dropping fire", a slave holding up his burning hand, a lion glaring at him and then walking by, "the bird of night ... sitting at the marketplace at noon". Casca draws the conclusion that the sum of all of these unusual occurrences must be signs of "civil strife in heaven"; he offers as an alternative interpretation: these are signs that the gods are taking revenge on humans because they have become too proud. This is the familiar archetypal fantasy of nemesis for hubris. As he says, "the world, too saucy with the gods, Incenses them to send destruction". The unusual, that which did not fit into the normal order of things, in other words, chaotic events in nature (considered a mirror of human life in pre-scientific cultures as well as in the Elizabethan culture), chaos was seen as an evil omen. There are, however, also cultures in which, for example, the unusual, like the birth of a deformed child has been considered a special, even a miraculous sign from the gods. This was the case in ancient Egypt and still is the case in parts of India to this day. Also in the contemporary Western world some religious communities interpret the birth of children with Down's syndrome as a gift from God.

The ambivalence of human reactions to the appearance of abnormal creatures with freakish bodies or monumental threatening hybrid creatures is basic to the phenomenology of humans facing what they consider as monsters. The aspect of warning, portent, in *monere* is not ubiquitous when encountering or rather developing fantasies about monsters. However, always present, as we shall see in more detail later, is the reference to another sphere – outside of, beyond the ordinary.

The characteristics of monsters

And now, to the characteristics: from Antiquity until today monsters are generally monumental, mostly frightening hybrid creatures combining various animal characteristics sometimes with human ones. Communication with them is practically impossible; they are isolated and seem to approach human beings with evil intent; they are powerful and destructive of human life. Therefore, they evoke fear, but they also evoke fascination; their emergence from another realm, which is definitely not human makes them impressive; one can even say that their appearance is numinous.

Polyphemus with his one eye, Medusa with her snake hair and deadly gaze, centaurs, the Hydra and the Sphinx all belong to the category of monsters that are threatening and fascinating hybrid creatures. The archetypal creative spirit has always produced hybrid creatures. Not all were necessarily threatening, but they were always unusually powerful. Already the Egyptian deities combined human and animal traits. But the first known example of a hybrid creature created by a human hand dates back to prehistoric times: the Lion Man of Ulm with his lion head and human body was made in approximately 40,000 BCE; the Venus of Hohle Fels is his contemporary; the Dancing Sorcerer from the Cave of the Trois-Frères in Ariège, France – with his human form, animal head, horns and tail and dancing on two of his four feet – is of much younger date: 14,000 BCE. These prehistoric figures can be considered zoomorphic or anthropomorphic creatures – hybrid. We do not know if they were threatening for prehistoric man, but they must have been powerful and impressive. Modern archaeologists consider them evidence of early mankind's spirituality and imagine that they were used in ritual contexts. Tribal customs till this day often adopt animal traits for their headdress or costume. The special characteristics of the animals chosen are meant to lend the animal's power to the tribesman. Tribes used the characteristics of animals as part of their identity, either in their dress, their personal names, their totem poles, etc.

The otherworldliness of monsters

I find it particularly interesting that monsters are so prevalent, actually we can say popular, in our times. We live in a rather secular period in history; in comparison with previous eras, spirituality plays a minimal role. Few contemporaries are religious; many are agnostics, atheists; people are also leaving established religious institutions in large numbers. And yet, or perhaps because of this, monsters are a popular topic in cinematic, comic and novel narratives. This can be seen as a compensatory manifestation of the collective unconscious: the traditional sphere of the numinous religious experience has been seriously questioned and on a large scale; it has even been rejected. Church and state are frequently separated; many modern societies go so far as to call themselves secular societies. The numinous is sought and arises in many other forms in contemporary life; natural beauty, extraordinary occurrences of many tones and flavours can all lead to very emotional moments that evoke in people a sense of thrill, a sense of the spiritual. The portrayal, however, of monsters from other realms who are greater than life size, even monumental, composite creatures, speaking another language or communicating in completely different ways make a serious impression on us, they can impress us, frighten us, thrill us. And they invariably point to some other realm of being with which we are not familiar, which does not belong to ours. They are monstrous, but are not necessarily deities, nor do they refer to deities. Their numinosity rather has more to do with their reference to some unknown civilisation to which men ascribe superiority. And hence, extra-ordinary power is common to all. Frightening, impressive and fascinating all at once, monsters are extra ordinary; they do not correspond with the realm of the norm and the normal. They represent chaos.

The power of the extra ordinary

We all feel, but do not consciously acknowledge our appreciation of the power of the extra ordinary. In his essay "The Structure of the Psyche" Jung noted, while speaking of the "mighty ancestor spirits dwelling in the man of importance" the "power residing in anyone strange or extraordinary" (Jung, 1927: para. 335). When societies choose, for example, the wounded, psychologically unstable, actually extraordinary person as a shaman they are tapping into these unusual peoples' power to contact other realms. In this

FIGURE 3.1 Anthropomorphic wooden statuette tibala carved by the Lobi people, Burkina Faso and Ivory Coast (height 24 cm)

Photo: Jean-Gilles Berizzi. Musée du quai Branly – Jacques Chirac © RMN-Grand Palais/Art Resource, NY

respect the Lobi tribe (originally from Ghana) is especially interesting. The Lobi form and offer up to their gods statuettes (Figure 3.1). When they are in need of very strong, phenomenally powerful help, in especially difficult life situations, they create statuettes that are in some way different, out of the ordinary, with unusual features – abnormal beings, like a man with one arm, or even two heads. The unusual is considered especially effective in combating great difficulty.

We know similar magical thinking when we remember the special power ascribed to the number 13 in the Western world. It is the uneven number that falls out of the totality of 12, normally grouped together as a dozen. Number 13 lies outside that ordinary order; it therefore represents and is believed also to provoke chaos, and therefore bad luck. Even luxurious hotels in modern megacities have no thirteenth floor, for example. But, the opposite is also true: for many people the number 13 brings luck. The fact is that it is powerful: for some people it causes good, for others evil. For the Lobi, the chaotic, the extra ordinary brings good luck.

Because of their power, monsters or creatures with monster-like features have been created to guard buildings – temples (dragon-like dogs), churches (gargoyles), bridges (Saint Christopher, who, according to legend, was originally a giant with a dog's head and came from a man-eating tribe).

Ambivalent reactions to monsters

The deep ambivalence of human reactions to monsters is beautifully illustrated in the movie *Godzilla*. First filmed in Japan in 1954 by Ishiro Honda, the movie has been remade 35 times. In the Japanese original the people, terrorised by the monster of the deep with its destructive radiation breath (nine years earlier the atomic bomb had been dropped on Hiroshima), flock to see him, awed by his monumentality, his strange form and his destructive powers. This pattern of reaction to monsters is a basic feature of all monster movies, which today are so extremely numerous and are often box office hits. New cinematic versions, not only of Godzilla, but also of Frankenstein and King Kong, continue to attract crowds, eager to experience the thrilling mixture of fear and fascination.

Creating monsters: an archetypal need?

Why do people worldwide and at all times create monsters? I believe we need to evoke fear, and more especially fear of the unknown, be it the unusual, the foreign, the abnormal, in order to try to conquer this fear. And we need to be able to imagine conquering the monster as heroes. Whoever says monster also says hero – from the slaying of the dragon to the conquest of the Sphinx and of Dr. No. The simplest everyday example is the child who, fearing the monster, dares to look under her bed.

The hero shares some of the monster's traits: he is not only extremely powerful, but he is also often of foreign origin. We can think in this connection of the many fairy tales and mythologies such as we have seen in Chapter 2, in which a stranger who suddenly appears on the scene is capable of rescuing a threatened civilisation. Many fairy tales and myths portray the stranger as the hero who fights the impossible fight, figures out the answer to the riddle which threatens the local population, saves the demoiselle in distress or the entire kingdom from destruction. This mytheme is so common that it is often overlooked. It plays an extremely important role in the psychotherapeutic process, as we shall see in the final chapter.

Beowulf is an early prototype of this theme. It has been taken up quite directly in the modern film *Outlander*. In the film the foreigner has extraordinary powers because of his strength and courage and also because of his special sword: made of a special metal that comes from his far away world, it is especially effective. He uses it to fight and ultimately defeat the monster Grendel. It is his foreign origin that makes him supremely capable of destroying the monster and rescuing the civilisation.

Superman is a modern mythological being representing the same theme. The cartoon figure was created in the United States in 1938 by a Jewish artist, Joe Shuster, and a Jewish writer, Jerry Siegel. He was a foreigner named Kal-El from the planet Krypton and was the sole sur-vivor of that planet. When his parents realised that the complete destruc-tion of their planet was imminent they sent their child to Earth on a space ship. On the level of the collective unconscious, Superman repre-sents the ideal and idealised hero who had to be created to combat the evil forces of the time, represented in the reality of the 1930s and 1940s by Adolf Hitler who was attempting to destroy any traces of non-Aryan life on planet Earth.

Ultimately, all man-made monsters actually seem to be beneficial. Encountering them brings about the beginning of a new universe, just as we shall see in a moment; on the individual level, newly acquired con-sciousness is the door to a new realm. But, in order for this transforma-tive process to take place the monster needs to be conquered by a hero. Therefore, the generally masculine hero (the first female superhero, Fan-tomah, was created in 1940) is an integral part of every monster story. Actually it is this couple – monster and hero – which is an archetypal pattern of experience.

Monsters and heroes: the development of consciousness

What makes the couple so fascinating that people throughout time have created so many such stories? I would like to look at two levels of interpretation here. First, the level of psychological development. It has been described in detail by Erich Neumann in his book *The Origins and History of Consciousness* (Neumann, 1954). Neumann considered the challenge and ultimate fight with and conquering of the monster by the hero a symbolisation of the evolution of consciousness out of the uroborus. The dragon monster represents the unconscious and the hero represents ego consciousness. This symbolic encounter and fight I see again and again in my practice where clients spontaneously choose some form of monster to represent the evil aspects of the mother or their entire primary family. In fact, the mother monster evoked by my clients is the destructive side of the Great Mother, criticising and mistreating, abusing her children, if not symbolically killing or eating them like Kali. She may also represent, as seen in my client's drawing in Chapter 5, the super-ego possessed mother who crushes the child with her accusations and labels it for life as unworthy. Overcoming this monster means developing beyond the realm of the dragon/undifferentiated unconscious with all of its unknown and frightening features. The goal is to find a higher level of consciousness and independence, a new realm of existence. And, as we know, this encounter is by far a one-time event. We continue throughout life to battle our monsters, especially our inner monsters.

Monster making and scapegoating

But let us look here at the societal level of the monster, what the monster phenomenon might represent on the level of society. As we have seen briefly in Chapter 1, xenophobic political parties project onto foreigners characteristics that we have seen as typical for monsters: speaking another language, they refer to another realm – their home country – and communication with them is difficult, if not impossible. In many ways they do not fit into the host society; they are invariably considered in some way powerful, but often in a negative, threatening sense. They may not be monumental in size but are considered monumental in numbers. Their numbers are always exaggerated. As discussed in Chapter 1, they can be seen as cooks or as crooks. If they do not manage to integrate well they are considered crooks, stealing from society – taking or attacking their women, taking their jobs and profiting from the host country's economy and social welfare benefits. The foreigner who, however, manages to integrate into the new society may remain a foreigner, but he can be powerful and fascinating in a positive sense, contributing to the host society in some positive manner, like becoming a good cook of some exotic kind of food.

More specifically ... anti-Semitism

I would like to look briefly at some common prejudices about Jewish people – in many societies considered the eternal foreigners. They have been accused of having both an extraordinary power and an extraordinary will to power: politically, socially and financially seeking control of the host society. During the Nazi period this was quite evidently a projection of the Nazis' plans to conquer the world. In his book *Der ewige Antisemit* (The Eternal Anti-Semite; my translation), Heinrich Broder cites the Reichstag representative Graf zu Reventlov who, in 1932, before an assembly, pronounced,

> Jews ... are incomparably superior, higher and more valuable than Germans ... In the face of this group chosen by their God we Germans feel inferior and hopelessly oppressed. It is unbearable for us to live side by side with such boundless perfection. We can only say from the depths of our inferiority, that so much divine light blinds us.
>
> *(Broder, 1986: 89; my translation)*

Communication with Jewish people is considered difficult. Despite the fact that the people speak the local language, participate in the local society as normal citizens and their houses of prayer are open and welcoming of the local population, this prejudice is unshaken. Fantasies about the group's size, its cohesiveness, its will to power and its wealth are truly of the realm of fantasy in the minds of the anti-Semitic community.

Many have tried to understand what makes Jewish people the perennial scapegoat, an object of hatred and envy. In her recent book on anti-Semitism, Delphine Horvilleur (2019: 22) points to the origin of the name of the Jewish people. In the Bible they are called Hebrews: the Hebrew word *ivri* means *he who crosses over*. The group is identified as one that does not remain in one place, but crosses over or migrates. It is unfortunately true that again and again in the course of history, the people are "in migration mode", first because of repeated prejudice, exclusion and persecution and the resulting lack of a homeland. In contrast, historically local in-groups have naturally claimed the right to enjoy local privileges such as owning land, living within the walls of the city, joining the local guilds. Exclusion from these rights created an existential situation, which singled out the group and its members as "them" and added to the basic perception and reality of their difference. In this manner negative projections have been facilitated.

The only other plausible explanation that I have found is the fact that on an archetypal level, new generations of gods tend to fight and attempt to destroy earlier generations of gods, as the Olympians did with the Titans. Succeeding generations in politics, especially in American politics, tend to do the same: whatever the Democrats have managed to accomplish during their term in office, the Republicans, when they win the following election, try to destroy. Jesus was of Jewish lineage and supposedly a member of one of the Jewish sects of his day, the Essenes. Like them, he propounded the values and mores of his sect, was accordingly critical of some of the more traditional forms of the religion. Although the Jews and the new Christians prayed together for centuries, with time the Church and the Synagogue separated. The enmity, of which there were definite signs beforehand, began. The religion of the past became the declared enemy and no longer an important source.

The underlying envy, which powered this destruction, was fed by the fantasies of the power of the people. On the one hand, seen as cooks, they were accused of being crooks – the flip side of the archetype of the foreigner.

Foreigners are easily projective surfaces for monster projections. This tendency can even find expression in iconography: during the Middle Ages Jews were portrayed as monstrous beings – half animal, with hooves and horns, sucking on pigs' teats. The monster projection is, on the collective level, clearly destructive. Here the reigning social order projects the characteristics of the monster onto a minority and then goes about trying to destroy it. The collective's identification with the hero is an act of hubris on the part of the society with its hegemonic value system. The foreigner is treated not as a *thou* but as an *it*, an inimical and powerful *it* that does not conform to the reigning social order and therefore represents chaos; it must be rejected – banned or destroyed. In the Hebrew Bible the scapegoat was sent out into the desert with the sins of the society loaded onto its head. In the symbolism of the monster, evil is projected onto the monster who is no longer just a goat, but a foreign minority – be it physically different, or not sharing the beliefs, the values, the ordering system of the majority of the society.

Can we find here a positive significance? Conquering the monster in the sense of removing the projections from the minority would mean a further developmental step. The projection of the shadow would be overcome; the hero society would have conquered the projection. The example of Marduk with Tiamat is a good illustration of what is then possible. The hero Marduk creates a new universe out of the body of the conquered mother monster Tiamat. A new world can be created through the removal of the projections. But, the foreigner monster cannot be stripped of the negative projections by the hero because the collective is not Marduk, not really a hero! I believe only individuals can manage this. Herein lies the most difficult aspect of the problem: the unconscious identification of the collective (its values, its reigning order) with the hero. The power of the herd makes a raising to consciousness of this act of hubris impossible: I will come back to this point in a moment.

New attitudes to monsters

Before I conclude these reflections on monsters, I must note that not all monsters are basically evil, especially modern monsters. Mary Shelley's monster only begins to attack people when his creator, Dr. Frankenstein, abandons him (Shelley, 1818/1981). The creature seeks to punish his creator for abandoning him. Nor is the Golem evil. He was created to protect the Jewish population. One version of the Golem myth even portrays him as only becoming a murderous monster when he feels rejected. King Kong is shown abducting a woman whom he loves and is trying to protect. This new idea of coming to appreciate the human aspects – their need for love and approval – of monsters is significant.

A recent film also tries to find a new approach to the hero–monster narrative. In *The Shape of Water* the monster is a large, aquatic hybrid creature from Brazil. He has been captured and brought to a scientific laboratory for experiments and is eventually to be killed. In this laboratory a mute cleaning woman finds a way to communicate with him: she feeds him apples and plays classical music recordings to him (otherwise, as we have seen, communication with monsters is difficult, even impossible). This outsider and her friends join together to save the monster. Outsiders are the topic of the film. All are different – out of the ordinary, do not belong to the society in which they live – but, the monster and the outsiders all have the same human needs. In this way the monster cannot be the scapegoat for them. Does this mean that in our times we can imagine encountering the monster in a more humane way? The 1990 film *E.T.* in which a cute creature from another planet is befriended and not attacked also pointed in this direction. In 1966 the Muppets on the television series *Sesame Street* featured a Cookie Monster. And most recently (2017) Emil Ferris wrote and illustrated her *My Favorite Thing Is Monsters*.

A 2015 role-playing video game called "Undertale" also portrays the situation of the monster with less unequivocal negativity. The player may choose how to deal with the monsters: he may or may not kill them and can win the game without killing any. Does this mean that in the modern world scapegoating could disappear, monster projections be removed from minorities?

Can the collective look under the bed and see that what is foreign is not necessarily dangerous? Trying to become acquainted with the foreigner could help him/her be seen more as a human being with differences, but with a lot of basic similarities. With time will monster stories disappear? Or, perhaps, they will become less frightening and more amenable to humane confrontation, as the Other, the foreign with which one can communicate.

As Julia Kristeva (1988) so clearly says, "the foreigner is within us"; the monster is also within us and we can all too easily project him/her onto the outside world. And, even if we manage to recognise and accept the foreign or even the monster within us, we are not necessarily open to the foreigner in the world. Jung's encounter with the foreign within himself did not prevent him from finding bizarre and even pathological the works of Picasso: "Picasso's psychic problems, so far as they find expression in his work, are strictly analogous to those of my patients" (Jung, 1932b: para. 205). As for James Joyce, whose *Ulysses* Jung re-evaluated in 1932 after having given up on it ten years previously, he finds it "no more a pathological product than modern art as a whole" (Jung, 1932a: para. 174). In the final chapter I shall be presenting case examples of the encounter with the foreigner/monster within.

Is scapegoating nevertheless somehow curable?

On the level of society, scapegoating – projecting the monster onto the minority group – is too widespread; it seems especially virulent at the present time; no cure has yet been found. The in-group seems to need to define its identity through the clear distinction between we and them. The phenomenon has been called a cultural complex. The most interesting aspect of a complex is not the mere fact that it exists. Everyone has some kind of mother or father complex; every society has some type of a cultural complex that is projected onto the foreign minority. I have never known a society which has not done so! But, the interesting question is always how the ego/the society deals with the complex: what is the feeling tone of the complex, is it more or less conscious. To repeat, how does the ego/society deal with the complex? Once faced with hardship, the insider group too often tends to project the causes of the hardship onto the foreigner group, the them – be they women (witches), homosexuals, Jews, blacks, and most recently, Muslims. The complex is intensely negative in tone – filled with fear, hatred, envy; the ego attempts to fight it, to get rid of it. Such shadow projections can grow to disproportionate sizes as one sees again and again in the course of history. Large amounts of energy can be devoted to fighting the complex of the foreign monster: entire armies and camps of all kinds, complex laws and administrative facilities can be created in order to exclude and ultimately exterminate the foreign monster.

On the level of the individual, such shadow projections are not unusual; they do not necessarily however take on the massive proportions that they tend to do in society. Here the power of the masses magnifies the energy of the projective phenomenon and, as social research has shown, it is infinitely more difficult for masses to come to consciousness.

In my experience as an analyst the only way that I have seen the removal of such projections is on the individual level. My sincere hope is that these individuals who have managed to remove negative projections onto others can become multiplicators, daring to warn and inform others of the danger of their projections. People are not monsters even if the power of the mob tends to see them that way.

References

Broder, Henryk M. (1986) *Der Ewige Antisemit: Über Sinn Und Funktion Eines Beständigen Gefühls*. Frankfurt am Main: Fischer Taschenbuch.

Exhibition Catalogue Museum Rietberg (1981) *Zürich Kunst Und Religion Der Lobi*. Zurich: Publikationsstiftung für das Museum Rietberg Zürich.

Ferris, Emil (2017) *My Favorite Thing Is Monsters*. Korea: Fantagraphics Books.

Horvilleur, Delphine (2019) *Réflexions Sur La Question Antisémite*. Paris: Grasset & Fasquelle.

Jung, C. G. (1927) 'The Structure of the Psyche'. *The Collected Works*, Vol. VIIIV (English Edition). Princeton, NJ: Princeton University Press.

Jung, C. G. (1932a) '"Ulysses": A Monologue'. *The Collected Works, Vol. XV* (English Edition). Princeton, NJ: Princeton University Press.

Jung, C. G. (1932b) 'Picasso'. *The Collected Works, Vol. XV* (English Edition). Princeton, NJ: Princeton University Press.

Kristeva, Julia (1988) *Étrangers À Nous-mêmes*. Paris: Gallimard.

Neumann, Erich (1954) *The Origins and History of Consciousness*. Princeton, NJ: Princeton University Press.

Shelley, Mary (1818/1981) *Frankenstein*. New York: Bantam.

Thorndike, S. (ed.) (1973) *The Complete Works of William Shakespeare*. London: Murrays Sales & Service C. Cresta House.

4

ALIENATION IN THE MODERN WORLD

Feeling foreign

Alienation

Alienation is a central topic for many twentieth-century writers – to mention only a few from different countries: Albert Camus, Thomas Mann and Paul Bowles. These writers delved into the problems and the personality of those who felt foreign in society, not connected with the world around them or with themselves. This is the population we are most often dealing with in psychotherapy.

Feeling one does not fit in is the plight of a large number of people at least since the Industrial Revolution when people became less closely and personally identified with their work and the society around them. The tribal worker knew for a fact that whatever he was making was meant for his tribe; he belonged to his group; his identity was defined by it. There was not an iota of doubt about his personal commitment to this tribe, to its safety and its wellbeing. Few are those in our world today who feel so identified with the society in which they live and with the work they do to support themselves and their family. Not being able to identify with his work and his family was one of the difficulties with which Kafka was dealing in his personal life and which served as the motif for *The Metamorphosis* (1916/2013), which I shall be discussing here.

One aspect that contributes to today's feelings of alienation is social mobility, not only within one's social class, but also from one place – one city, one country – to the other. The French language uses the word "*dépaysement*" to describe a state of disorientation, in which a person does not feel orientated to himself or feels estranged. The word actually refers, however, to the country from which one comes: *pays* means country.

Literally, *dépaysement* means not feeling as in one's country or not feeling at home. The extreme frequency of social mobility undoubtedly presents a tremendous challenge to the individual whose identity is no longer a matter of fact given by the society to which he belongs. This physical fact of modern life contributes to the widespread feelings of alienation today and, of course, contributes to the cosmopolitan nature of the world. People today are often what we call "cultural hybrids", coming from one culture, living in another and identifying perhaps with still another due to their family's origins.

As we have seen in Chapter 2, Moses is a very early example of a young man who can actually be called a cultural hybrid. He felt his foreignness and sought a sense of belonging and appreciation in the society of the Hebrews. He committed himself to a cause that could favour his acceptance by the group to which he yearned to belong. Too often, young people in particular can join a cause which promises them more rapid fulfilment of the archetypal needs that the new society in which they find themselves cannot so quickly fulfil. Of course, what I am not considering here is the personal level, the inner psychic aspects that obviously also shape the development of any human being: the early years in the family and, especially in the case of the refugee, the inevitable traumatisation of the individual through those difficult life events. These aspects must not be ignored, but, when dealing with archetypal phenomena, such questions are not at the centre of our attention.

I would like to look at the perspective of the foreigner himself, taking as my first example a group of Islamists whose struggles in dealing with their feelings of alienation, feeling foreign in society (be it that of other Muslims who do not adhere so strictly to the rules of the religion, or that of the surrounding non-Muslim society) often lead to violence.

Salafist terrorists

It might seem strange to begin a discussion of the topic of present-day alienation with the example of terrorists; nevertheless, this extreme example does indicate important aspects of the general phenomenon.

The Salafists, a group of Islamic fundamentalists who believe in the jihad to which they aspire, are taught to prize their own foreignness, which otherwise, in everyday life, causes them suffering. They are often but not always foreigners in foreign lands; sometimes they just feel foreign/alienated. They suffer from the fact that their archetypal needs for belonging and appreciation are not fulfilled by the society in which they live. The fundamentalist ideology cunningly transforms the foreigner label to make it feel positive: they call themselves "*Gharieb*", meaning foreigners, because, from their point of view, their strict understanding and observance of Islamic laws sets them apart from the rest of Muslim society. In joining the group, which commits to perform the jihad, its members are promised a sense of belonging, meaning and fulfilment. One of their battle songs (composed in 1985 by Saad al-Ghamidi) is called "*Ghurabaa*", "Foreigners" or "Strangers". It is a "*nasheed*", a piece of Islamic musical culture, praising the Salafist for being different.

The text is often sung with the refrain "strangers, strangers, strangers". It declares that the life motto of the group is the choice of being different from others. As the group is devoted only to Allah, its members pray to and obey only him; they are happy to be strangers to the rest of the world. As they will always be only Allah's soldiers, they will declare allegiance to no other political leaders. They reject any other way of being; this is the path that they have chosen. They do not care if they are thrown into prison because of this choice: theirs is the path of resistance. Their intention is to commit jihad: they want to fight. They actually feel free in a world that tries to enslave them. They often recall their happy moments spent reading and reciting the words of Mohammed morning and night. They bow to no one except Allah.

The text refers to a thirteenth-century hadith, a commentary of Islam, by Abu Huraira, who was a companion of Mohammed and known for his hadiths; their authenticity has been questioned. Abu Huraira reports that the messenger of Allah said that Islam began as something strange or foreign and it would once again be strange or foreign; therefore, strangers are blessed. Because of this strangeness, in the sense of originality, Islam began as a new and different way of life; Mohammed's followers are necessarily also strange. (In Chapter 2 we have seen the importance of the new and foreign in all new religious ideas.) This reversal in the evaluation of their situation as foreigners is naturally very appealing to those who are used to seeing themselves as the victims, even the losers in society, looked down upon for being foreigners, and, consequently, not being allowed to become respected and successful and members of the new society. The message of this hadith suggests that the victim pole of the archetypal experience of being the foreigner can be reversed to the hero pole.

So, the Salafists underline the positive power of their difference, compensating for their everyday negative feeling of unimportance and inferiority as foreigners. In his work, as we shall see in more detail further on in this chapter, the psychologist Ahmad Mansour offers Muslim youth a forum in which they can discuss their situation, become more aware of their difficulties and attempt to find other solutions. A forum of this kind is a place where fertilisation can occur and lay the ground for positive transformational processes. Of course, the surrounding society must also try to help these people find a way of fulfilling their archetypal needs. When the socio-political system manages to provide perspectives for further development and integration, the people can feel less hopeless and rejected as foreigners, and the less likely they will be open to joining a radical group.

Albert Camus and Meursault

The topic of the foreigner is the title of Camus' novel (*L'Étranger*), first published in 1942, during the German occupation of France; the work is considered a prime example of the novel of the absurd. I find it interesting to note that the first English-language translation – in Britain – was called *The Outsider*; in America it was called *The Stranger*. Camus himself was an outsider: he grew up in a poor family in Algeria. His family had settled there three generations earlier. His father, who grew up in Algeria, was enlisted in the French army and was killed in France during the First World War, when Camus was one year old. His mother, of Spanish origin, was an illiterate woman who, on the death of her husband, took her two little boys and moved in with her own mother and her uncle. She worked first in a factory and then as a domestic in order to support her family. Her own mother, a strict penny-pinching woman, became the boss of the household. Camus speaks of his mother as the only woman he ever loved; his desire for her love and terrible guilt feelings for having left her in Algeria and gone off to France marked him. He speaks very clearly of this guilt in his autobiography, *Le Premier Homme* (1994/ 2000), which was found in the wreckage of the car in which he was killed in 1960 and which was published posthumously (in 1994) by his daughter. Here he described his mother as silent, showing little interest in the world around her other than looking out the window (to watch whatever was happening on the street) and little interest in her child. Despite his intellectual abilities, Camus was always an outsider; this began already when he started school, as he was incapable of speaking proper French. Again and again his grandmother tried to prevent him from pursuing his studies: he was meant to work to help support the family; this he did – begrudgingly, because he loved the beach, the sun and football – during vacation time. Beside the poverty and the lack of a supportive background, Camus had serious health problems and had several serious, life threatening bouts of tuberculosis, which forced him to give up his beloved football and to interrupt his university studies. These various aspects of his personal situation made Albert Camus especially sensitive to the question of not belonging. Of course, being the son of a French man living in Algeria he also knew the phenomenon of exclusion from the other perspective. Camus spoke of people of Arab descent merely as "the Arabs". This seeming derision also plays a role in *L'Étranger*.

But, Meursault, the main figure and narrator, seems not to belong to the world around him in other ways. He generally does not openly express emotions and is seen by the surrounding world as being so unemotional, so emotionally distant as not to fit into the normal world. The few times he does show feelings are at the end of the novel, for example, when he gets angry at the priest who is trying to comfort him and then, shortly afterwards rejoices in the fantasy that the crowd that witnesses his execution will shout their hatred toward him.

This foreigner does not fit in because of his emotional detachment, his alienation from society. He does not seem to suffer from this attitude: it is his identity – not to be involved emotionally with the world around him. And this is what makes him capable of shooting the Arab stranger he meets on the beach. Meursault's emotional detachment seems to echo that which Camus himself describes as his mother's attitude. According to his German biographer, Iris Radisch (2013), even when her son died she merely said, "That is too young", turned round and continued looking out the window as she always did. She died that same year.

Meursault is a stranger – an outsider would be the preferable description – who does not feel helpless: he fits in where, when and how he wants to. And this raises the question of the absurd: the term does not perhaps refer to the surrounding world, to the society with its clear value codes that do not allow for diverse identities and diverse modes of adapting to these codes. Meursault's indifference is that of Camus himself, the outsider who learned to detach himself emotionally from the surrounding world in order not to suffer from his exclusion from society.

Toward the end of his relatively short life, Albert Camus continued living life as he saw fit, seemingly not much differently from the way Meursault seems to have lived. He lived a kind of social murder, sent into social exile, excluded from the world of French intellectuals by Jean-Paul Sartre who had been full of praise for *L'Étranger*, but in 1952 wrote excruciatingly critical and cruel pages of criticism against Camus. After this 19-page article few continued to associate with and appreciate Camus and his work. History has corrected that: Camus received the Nobel Prize for Literature in 1957; his *The Outsider* has become a major work illustrative of the phenomena of human alienation. In recent years it has been considered the portrait of Asperger's syndrome.

In fact, in psychotherapy, we work with people who feel they do not belong and withdraw from society because of their pain; however, as I mentioned in the beginning of this discussion, Meursault does not seem to suffer from not belonging. Camus' mother Catherine may have been so distant because of a need to retreat from the world due to traumatic life experiences, which she could not digest. Camus himself never admitted to his own suffering, but biographical information seems to point to depressive phases from which he tried to escape by hypomanic behaviour. These hypotheses are obviously difficult to verify. For our discussion here biographical information seems to show that the feelings of alienation described in *L'Étranger* are directly related to the personal life of its author and have to do with many factors – family circumstances, his primary relationship, early life experiences, his health issues, poverty and migration.

Franz Kafka and Gregor Samsa

I find Kafka's *The Metamorphosis* (1916/2013) a paradigmatic example of one type of modern foreigner's struggle and potential transformation. On the basis of this example I will go on to present the story of a real man today whose process echoes that of Kafka himself. This example, I believe, can help us appreciate the psychological situation of certain foreigners in our world today.

Kafka's sense of not belonging, his sense of alienation from others in the world around him, and from society in general, is apparent throughout his entire work. The three-volume biography by Reiner Stach (2002) shows ample proof of this. But, unlike Meursault, Kafka and his hero Gregor Samsa, the narrator and main character of *The Metamorphosis*, did not feel comfortable in their identity. We know that Kafka felt uncomfortable in his body and was constantly trying to improve his relationship with it; nor could he entertain a healthy relationship with a woman, either psychologically or sexually. Kafka and the hardly disguised fictional antihero Gregor Samsa rather felt like some kind of a lowly insect, which can, and in the novel also explicitly will, be disposed of. Kafka's low sense of self-esteem and the accompanying fear of rejection he describes in detail in the story of Gregor Samsa. One biographical explanation for this self-doubt he also explains in his *Letter to Father* (1919/1987) in which his father's physically imposing stature, and actually his entire being, make the boy Kafka shrink into a puny little creature. Although Kafka himself was not thrown on the garbage heap like Gregor, he wished that all of his writing be destroyed on his death.

The Metamorphosis describes a man who feels alienated from himself and from society. As he wrote in a letter to Carl Bauer (the father of his fiancée Felice Bauer), on August 28, 1913, he felt more foreign than a foreigner amid his family. He clearly identified with the central character of his novella, Gregor Samsa. Kafka himself spent the mornings writing before he went off to work at an insurance company. The wages he earned allowed him to pay his bills and those of his family. He did not feel at home in himself, neither in his body, in his work nor in his family. This is exactly the same situation as Gregor Samsa: also an adult man who lives at home with his family of origin; he works as a travelling salesman in order to help his father pay his debts. When, however, Gregor Samsa goes through his transformational process, living his alienation to the point of becoming an insect, he becomes conscious of his state. And, as a bug – lying awkwardly in his human bed – he reflects on his life and his estrangement from it.

Becoming a bug, and finally being completely rejected and ending up on a garbage heap, led to the hopeless, the definitive end of the life of Gregor Samsa. This is also how the story ends; however, *The Metamorphosis* is seen today as one of the greatest literary masterpieces of the twentieth century. The garbage heap on which the main character ends up can actually be considered a place of fertilisation. Gregor Samsa's destiny – and that of his creator who so clearly identified with Gregor – is actually to become an immortal literary personality! Unfortunately, neither of them lived to experience this transformation. But, one hundred years later we can give testimony to the fact that a remarkable literary work emerged. It was Kafka's personal, extremely emotional testimony. Like *The Judgment*, which was written in one night in 1912, *The Metamorphosis* was written very quickly (from November to December of 1912). Although he was not as enthusiastic about this work as about the former, Kafka felt that the realisation and fictional description of his alienation was essential for his further development; soon after writing the novella (August 1914) he finally managed to leave home, on the surface for practical reasons – his sister moved in and took his room. Kafka's conscious realisation and description of his alienation helped him find somewhat more satisfying solutions for his personal life. Kafka, the completely alienated, suffering human being, who feels foreign in his own skin becomes the example par excellence of the artist foreigner and an immortal author.

A modern man and the flip side of the archetype

Now, I would like to present a real-life story of a transformational process. It is the story of a young man, who identified with the poor, underprivileged victim-foreigner, considering himself a social reject; he was on his way to becoming a criminal-foreigner, a crook, actually an Islamist. I had the privilege of hearing Ahmad Mansour speak at a conference in Frankfurt in 2017; he spoke there of his development, his transformational process. In his first book, *Generation Allah* (2015) he describes his development. In his most recent book (*Klartext zur Integration*, 2018), he tells his story in a more intimate manner, narrating in detail his feelings of foreignness, the difficulties he faced when he came to Germany as a foreign student, his struggles with the language, with the mentality and his difficulty in becoming part of the culture which he had chosen. He felt foreign, helpless and excluded here.

Ahmad Mansour was born into a poor, unreligious Palestinian family in a small village in Israel. He suffered from the violence of his surroundings, sexual taboos, mobbing, fear; he felt insecure and had a poor sense of self-esteem. He did not feel that he fit in in the surrounding world, which did not tolerate any kind of independent thinking. He felt alone and had no hope for the future, found no meaning in his life. Then, the local Imam who taught at his school, spoke to him, encouraging him, telling him that he had great potential. The words of this impressive authority figure made him feel very special: he had been "chosen". He began attending the local mosque regularly, was invited to special Koran teachings. This was a turning point in Ahmad Mansour's life; he was no longer the outsider, but belonged to a community, which gave his life a sense of meaning outside of his patriarchal family. He felt secure in the mosque and with the community he met there. But the Imam slowly tried to indoctrinate him to Islamism: he painted a picture of the world in which Muslims were victimised, needed to take revenge and Islamise the world.

After graduating from high school Ahmad went to university in Israel and it was there that he went through his process of transformation. I do not know if you can consider a university a garbage heap, but it definitely is a place where fertilisation and transformation can take place. At university Ahmad became acquainted with new ideas; in his Frankfurt lecture he underlined the fact that he was actually most impressed by the atmosphere of intellectual freedom he met with in the psychology seminars – quite far from the dogmatic views he had heard from his Imam. He studied psychoanalytic texts and became a psychologist. In 2004 he immigrated to Germany where he now works with young Muslims (some of whom have already become radicalised, others who are tempted by it) and their families, trying to help them find a way to accept their foreignness in a creative, enriching manner instead of taking revenge for it in a destructive manner. He is one of Germany's leading experts on Islamism and radicalisation, working on projects to fight extremism and promote tolerance and democracy. He is also Programme Director at the European Foundation for Democracy and has been awarded many prizes for his work.

Ahmad Mansour's story can be considered a case of conversion as described in the New Testament story of the conversion from Saulus to Paulus; this is what, in Jungian theory, we would call a case of enantiodromia (Jung, 1920). His was a transformational process like that of Gregor Samsa–Kafka. From the passive, powerless, meaningless pole of the archetype, Kafka and Ahmad Mansour emerged to the cook pole: the creative foreigner who contributes to society.

Thomas Mann and Tonio Kröger

Tomas Mann's novella *Tonio Kröger* (1903) is, like the two literary works we have looked at above, autobiographical. Tonio Kröger's sense of not belonging can be felt to represent the plight of the artist in society, that is, outside of society. Tonio Kröger grew up in a rich merchant family in the north of Germany. His mother especially did not fit in physically: she was a dark-haired Spanish woman: this was a problem for Tonio as a young boy. And then there was his first name, in no way typically German or north German, but reflecting something more southerly, like his mother's roots. The boy wanted to belong, to have friends, the friends he wished for, whom he admired, who were the "in crowd", who were popular. Tonio felt different for all of these reasons. Not feeling understood in the society in which he grew up, he turned to writing poetry – a way in which he must have sought companionship with his inner world. It was at least a way in which Tonio could express himself and contact or communicate with other aspects of his personality. In this way he hoped to somehow feel less foreign. This led to Tonio's dilemma – constantly torn between his desire to belong to the bourgeois world of his origins and to escape from it.

When he grows up, Tonio does become a writer and does escape, settling in Munich in southern Germany. But the writer Tonio Kröger does not really feel that he belongs to the world of the artist either. This becomes quite apparent in a conversation with Lisaweta, a painter friend, in Munich. After a long and desperate monologue on the subject of his dissatisfaction with art and how it cannot really touch the bourgeois, Lisaweta explains very succinctly, "The answer is that you, just as you are sitting there, are a simple bourgeois!" (Mann, 1903: 177; my translation). "You are a bourgeois who is lost!", she adds. Tonio feels completely done in and decides to set out on a journey to his place of origin.

There he comes very close to being arrested for being a criminal and has difficulty proving his identity as he has no papers with him. He can only stammer that he is a writer and finally manages to persuade the police officer of his identity. During this entire voyage Tonio Kröger is preoccupied with his yearning for the bourgeois life he had known, realising on the one hand that he no longer belonged there, and on the other hand that he never really had belonged there, as he had always been different: even in those days he had devoted his energies to trying to fit in with the locals and writing poetry. None of his friends showed any interest in this activity. On his return from this voyage to his roots, he explains to Lisaweta:

> I stand between two worlds. I am at home in neither, and I suffer in consequence. You artists call me a bourgeois, and the bourgeois try to arrest me. I don't know which makes me feel worse.
>
> *(Mann, 1903: 214–215; my translation)*

Tonio Kröger is a foreigner within society and always was because he felt different, did not feel that he fit in with people around him, with what they were or what they expected of themselves, of him and life in general. This is one of the aspects of feeling foreign with which we deal in the analytical process.

The parallels between Tonio and Thomas are quite apparent. According to Kurzke (1999/2006), the writer grew up in Lübeck, Northern Germany in a wealthy German family. His mother was Spanish. When his father died the family moved south to Munich. But there is another dimension to this feeling like an outsider, which is not necessarily so apparent in reading the novella. The writer Thomas Mann suffered from a sense of alienation, the source of which is not presented as the central problem in the novella. It has to do with homosexuality. Tonio Kröger expresses clear interest in a young boy at school whom he would like to befriend more than this male object of his affections would like. Feeling misunderstood, not accepted in this relationship, he turned to writing. Thomas Mann himself was preoccupied with his homoerotic tendencies, which have come to light in his journals, some of which he did not destroy in his final home in California and were published posthumously. This feeling of not belonging, alienation, from the so-called normal world of heterosexual citizens was obviously difficult for the writer to manage. In certain of his works the main character shows a definite fascination with young men. In *Death in Venice*, the writer Gustav von Aschenbach actually falls in love with the young Polish boy Tadzio; he observes him with his family from afar during a vacation in Venice. It is quite apparent that Thomas Mann was especially concerned with keeping this deviation from society secret, as seen in the act of burning his meticulously kept journals at the end of his life. His homoerotic tendencies were one of the main sources of Mann's feelings of alienation; he carefully described the feelings while keeping their source as secret as possible.

Pictorial representations of alienation

Luncheon in the Studio, a painting by Edouard Manet (Figure 4.1) is a nineteenth-century artistic expression of the topic of alienation.

In *Luncheon in the Studio* (1868), the painter places three individuals so that, although they are in the same room, and are sharing the same space (supposedly the artist's own studio), each is clearly in his own personal space, separate from the others. They occupy three different planes. Up front a young man is seen almost in his entirety, looking out somewhere into space. To his right, coming from further back in the room, is a woman bringing in a coffee pot, not looking anywhere in particular. To the young man's left, sitting at the table in between the two planes, a male figure is smoking a cigar and gazing approximately in the direction of the young man. Each is occupying a different plane; each is looking in a different direction.

This is not a group portrait, but rather a snapshot of a moment in time in which three individuals occupying the same space are separated – can we say estranged? – from each other. Each seems preoccupied with his or

FIGURE 4.1 *Luncheon in the Studio* by Edouard Manet

Bayerische Staatsgemäldesammlungen bpk Berlin (Bavarian State Painting Collections). Used with permissions.

her own inner world. It is impossible to know what relationship they might have with each other; art historians have long debated this question. Is this Leon Keoella Leenhoff, thought to be either Manet's son or his half-brother? Is this Manet himself or rather his friend Auguste Rousselin? Is this a servant or perhaps Manet's wife Suzanne Leenhoff and the mother of the boy? These relationships, according to Manet's biographers, were complicated and have never been clarified. Does the painting refer to an unclear relationship situation or does it portray a moment of estrangement in which the males were in disagreement about something serious or something banal? Or is the boy just in a bad mood and unreachable for the moment? Discord, estrangement is definitely palpable, but the reason is in no way obvious.

It is significant that each of them has their own physical stance: the older man sitting at the table smoking a cigar, the woman entering to serve coffee, the young man leaning against the table in the front. One can well imagine that this disjointed placement of the figures symbolises how each has her own stance, her own opinion, her own point of view. They seem to be strangers to each other at this moment in time. Is there a hint that they have argued – in the helmet placed on the table –, that the atmosphere has turned sour – the lemon lying on the table? Communication no longer seems possible: in some way they have turned away from each other: a strange foreignness, a feeling of not really belonging together prevails. This is a far cry from group portraits of painters in the past; I am thinking here, for example, of portraits of royal families painted by Velazquez. This group scene most resembles Manet's own painting *The Balcony* where one also gets the impression of estrangement because the three figures on the balcony are all turned away from each other.

Of course, among more modern painters, Edward Hopper is seen as the painter par excellence of urban alienation. Any one of his rooms showing people alone gazing out of a window onto a concrete city landscape (Figure 4.2) so terrifyingly well depicts the topic that there is hardly need for discussion.

Hopper himself always denied that he was interested in the topic: he was merely interested in the special type of glaring light that floods these pictures. Nevertheless, the fact is that we see no hints of human relationships in the majority of his paintings, neither in his bar scene (*Nighthawk*), his gas stations, nor his people basking in the sun in lounge chairs, all facing in the same direction. Inevitably the models he portrays are individual people who are generally alone, isolated, seemingly estranged from others. The light is glaring. This adds to a certain kind of unpleasant atmosphere that bathes the scene and deftly evokes feelings of estrangement.

FIGURE 4.2 *Office in a Small City* by Edward Hopper
© Heirs of Josephine N. Hopper/VAGA at ARS, NY/VG Bild-Kunst, Bonn 2019. Used with permissions. The Metropolitan Museum of Art, Image copyright © The Metropolitan Museum of Art. Image source: Art, Resource, NY.

The personal unconscious or reductive analysis

In none of the above examples is it possible to get involved in and illustrate in a serious manner the deeper, personal levels of the experience of alienation. Without direct communication with the people themselves, one can only suppose, hypothesise about the personal unconscious. The following chapter devoted to the psychotherapeutic process can and will get involved in this other layer also, that of the personal unconscious or reductive analysis.

References

Camus, Albert (1957) *L'Étranger*. Paris: Gallimard.
Camus, Albert (1994/2000) *Le Premier Homme*. Paris: Gallimard.
Jung, C. G. (1920) 'Psychological Types'. *The Collected Works, Vol. VI* (English Edition). Princeton, NJ: Princeton University Press, para. 709.
Kafka, Franz (1916/2013) *The Metamorphosis* (trans. by K. Hasenpusch). New York: Crown Publishing Group.
Kafka, Franz (1919/1987) *Letter to Father*. New York: Schocken.

Kurzke, Hermann (1999/2006) *Thomas Mann: Das Leben Als Kunstwerk. Eine Biographie.* München: C. H. Beck.

Mann, Thomas (1963) 'Tonio Kröger' (first published in 1903). *Erzählungen: Ausgewählt Von Walter Jens* (Bibliothek des 20. Jahrhunderts), eds. Walter Jens and Marcel Reich-Ranicki, Stuttgart and Munich: Deutscher Bücherbund.

Mansour, Ahmad (2015) *Generation Allah: Warum Wir Im Kampf Gegen Religiösen Extremismus Umdenken Müssen.* Frankfurt am Main: S. Fischer Verlag. Bundeszentrale für Politische Bildung.

Mansour, Ahmad (2018) *Klartext Zur Integration: Gegen Falsche Toleranz Und Panikmache.* Frankfurt am Main: S. Fischer Verlag.

Radisch, Iris (2013) *Camus: Das Ideal Der Einfachheit.* Hamburg: Rowohlt Taschenbuch.

Stach, Reiner (2002, 3rd edition 2014) *Kafka: Die Jahre Der Entscheidungen.* Frankfurt am Main: Fischer Taschenbuch.

5

THE ENCOUNTER WITH THE FOREIGNER IN THE PSYCHOTHERAPEUTIC CONTEXT

Introduction

As we have seen in the preceding chapters, the encounter with the foreign Other in the outside world can be perceived as a challenge, met with various emotional reactions – from trepidation to fear, from curiosity to fascination. The same is true of the encounter with the foreigner within. This is the subject of depth psychology. The foreigner whom we call the unconscious can be felt as a challenge to the customary attitude; rather than the client's original attitude of rejecting the foreigner within, we try to encourage acceptance and integration.

So many of my clients have been foreigners: expatriates who left their country of origin for a certain more or less limited period of time for the sake of work or love; children and grandchildren of immigrants; recent urbanites, for example the children of farmers or other country people who moved to the city for better work opportunities. However, these self-willed, voluntary "strangers in a strange land" suffer a fate that they did not reckon with and which often causes insecurity and pain. I have worked with relatively few recent immigrants, but with many of their children and grandchildren. I also work with people who have been labelled as Other because of their not fitting in, be it through their unusualness – through their behaviour or appearance, a visible or audible handicap or even their belonging to a different religious or cultural group than the local majority. Still other clients in a moment of crisis catch a glimpse of a foreigner – an unknown Other – within themselves, a part of them who is perhaps not so strong and capable, competent, caring, self-sacrificing, as the person they had imagined themselves to be. All of these psychologically moving experiences are basically moments of alienation. They can be more or less unsettling for the individual concerned. I shall be exploring some of these cases here.

The foreigner within

Jung called the various nodal points of the personality the complexes, and even referred to them as "splinter psyches". We all have various aspects of our personality with which we identify, others of which we are less aware and still others that we want to have nothing to do with. As long as we are alive we have foreigners within us: we can never be omniscient about ourselves, or about anything or anyone else for that matter.

The little statuette shown in Figure 5.1 is from the Teotihuacan culture, which flourished in an area of Mexico north-east of Mexico City from around 100 BCE to 550 CE. Neither archaeologists nor ethnologists have been able to ascertain what this kind of statuette (many examples of which have been found, mainly in the graves of the Teotihuacan) meant to the people of that culture. It is a statuette in two halves: the top half represents a human being in a sitting position. The bottom half of the statuette is the back of the person. Inside this half we find many little faces or masks. I like to think that the way the Teotihuacans represented the inside of the human being shows that these people were aware of the fact that human beings are composed of many varying aspects, various facets, personalities which are

FIGURE 5.1 Teotihuacan host figurine
Photo by Ian Mursell/Mexicolore

not immediately apparent. From the outside people might seem to be one indivisible whole. They might not show their other sides (shadow aspects); they are probably not even aware of these aspects themselves – they are unconscious. This little sculpture, which I discovered at an exhibition of the Teotihuacan culture in the Rietberg Museum in Zurich often helps me explain to clients that they have many aspects to their personality, that they belong to them, in their entirety. Jung made a very simple but enlightening statement about the process of psychotherapy. He said that at the end of the process a person is "much more rounded and complete" (Jung, 1944/1952: para. 84), because he/she discovers other aspects of their personality: they learn to become aware of, accept and integrate other less conscious, even less acceptable sides of their personality. One can also formulate this as the discovery of the as yet unknown foreigners within, i.e. the unconscious.

Feeling foreign and discovering the foreigner within

Sonja Marjasch, who was one of my very inspiring teachers and an extraordinarily creative listener, wrote a paper on the difference between the "dream ego" and the "ego in dreams". She called the foreigner within, the "dream ego" (Marjasch, 1961) – an ego figure who represents to the dreamer but behaves in a different manner from the waking ego. In contrast, the "ego in dreams" acts as the waking ego would. In Jung's terminology we would speak of the shadow, which is not always a negative aspect of the personality, but can just as well be an unknown facet of the personality. It is in this way that the motif of the foreigner, as discussed in the preceding pages, is always symbolic of the Other, as yet unknown aspects of the personality. The appearance of this foreign element is provoked by the self-regulating psyche, guided by the Self with the intent of encouraging the individual to individuate, helping her potential to unfold so that she can become the unique individual that she is.

Gerry's story

The client about whom I want to speak now – I will call him Gerry – consulted me because he was afraid of contracting AIDS, which at that time was incurable. Tall, thin, handsome, Gerry was very shy. He was a gentle man who loved opera and art museums. He had a long-time partner with whom he had an open relationship: both of them indulged in outside adventures from time to time.

Gerry had had no higher education and was not used to talking, especially not about himself. In our initial sessions I often wondered if we would be able to work together: could Gerry open up to Frau Dr., to communicate with me? In my practice it was unusual for a client not to have a higher education. My suspicion proved to be entirely wrong. At the end of our work Gerry was one of the most conscious clients with whom I have ever worked. But more of this later.

Gerry had grown up in a home in which his mother held the sceptre; his father worked hard and was seldom home. When at home, he would rest on the living room couch and Gerry would bounce on him or sit beside him. Gerry loved his father who, through no fault of his own, could not spend time with his child. Gerry's mother was strict and quite brutal toward her only son: beatings and humiliation were the rule. At school also Gerry was bullied. Teachers shamed him, calling him stupid; he had black and blue marks all over his body from the beatings at home. He felt different, excluded; at some point he realised that he preferred boys. At that period in time this preference meant automatic ridicule and exclusion. Although it was no longer illegal to have homosexual relationships, homosexuality was considered seriously trespassing against society's values: it was completely taboo.

Obviously, Gerry felt very much the outsider, the foreigner; already as a child at home he had felt helpless, weak, insecure, unappreciated and excluded. And then, experiencing bullying in school deepened his feelings of not belonging – not belonging anywhere. On a deeper psychological level Gerry most likely did not know "the gleam in the mother's eye", which Heinz Kohut described as the basis for a stable sense of self-esteem; loving approval had been absent from his early days on. So, his foreignness, his feeling of not belonging had its roots in infancy and could not easily be overcome.

I think that the positive transference that developed with Gerry had much to do with one early positive, trusting relationship, which he had known: the relationship with his father's mother. This special kind of relationship with a grandparent is often helpful with clients who have had only this one positive relationship experience in their childhood. Luckily, many of my clients have had a loving grandmother who made up for some of the loving and appreciation the child had otherwise been lacking. Gerry spent a lot of time with his grandmother; she babysat for him when his parents were at work. She loved the little boy, cooked and baked with him; she was calm, loving and understanding. It is no wonder that Gerry grew up to become a gifted and well-acclaimed baker.

When he came to see me, Gerry had found a place in which he had a sense of belonging, a nest. It was his relationship with John that gave him this feeling. They shared the same interests – in opera, museums and travel; they loved and cared for each other. He gained the appreciation and joy that he had been missing as a child through his profession as

a baker; in his mind he was always but an apprentice of his loving grandmother. What remained from his past was the insecurity, the fear of
being vulnerable, so vulnerable that he could die. The fear that had
clearly originated in his early years was compounded by the realistic fact
that AIDS was rampant and incurable at that time.

Gerry was a generous person, intent on being appreciated by others.
This made it difficult, practically impossible, for him to make demands
on others: he tended to comply with the desires of those around him
rather than asking for anything, always hoping to find their appreciation.
This kind of reticence also prevented Gerry from asking John to refrain
from his sexual adventures, or at least not to engage in them without at
least some protection.

In the work with Gerry we find, as we shall see below, the appearance
of a helpful inner figure in a dream. This is also an encounter with
a foreigner, an unconscious aspect of the personality, which is positive. It
belongs to the shadow, in the sense of the unconscious, which, according
to Jungian psychology contains not only repressed, negative material, but
also potential for development. This is Gerry's dream, which became
a turning point in our work:

One night, Gerry dreamt that he had robbed a bank; on awakening he
was shocked. He could never do anything like that! It was against the
law; it was not right! The fantasy of demanding – at gunpoint! – something, that definitely did not correspond to Gerry's self-image; in fact it
was the extreme opposite of Gerry's conscious ego standpoint.

But his "dream ego" was of an entirely different opinion. In the
dream Gerry the bank robber was absolutely elated at his successful rob-
bery. The decalage between his emotional reactions in the dream and
then on awakening was a big surprise for Gerry. Asking about feelings in
and after dreams often reveals important material.

Acting out the robber unconsciously in the dream shows Gerry's
potential for being more demanding. Although he would never consciously have identified with this bank robber, the discovery of this foreigner within was indeed quite a beneficial shock for Gerry. It seemed as
though the character trait of the robber in some way needed to be integrated. I spent some time trying to explain to Gerry that whatever happened in the dream was actually his own, a fantasy of his own which
appeared in the night. Nighttime fantasies, I explained, are in general less
acceptable for us than daytime fantasies. And I suggested that whatever
the robber represented was a potential, an aspect of who he could be
and on some deeper level actually was. When he managed – to a certain
extent – to accept this new stance, Gerry became more open and direct
with John and did manage to have that conversation that was meant to

save both of their lives. Unfortunately, before the conversation could take place John had already been infected with the disease.

Soon after this conversation John was diagnosed; Gerry cared for him during the two years of his illness. When John died, Gerry made an appointment to see me. He told me what had happened and that he knew that he would probably die soon: he had some suspicious-looking symptoms, which the local clinic could not yet diagnose. According to what he had read about AIDS, these were some of the unusual initial symptoms of the illness. We saw each other regularly during this time. AIDS was then diagnosed.

Gerry was intent on continuing our work together. In these weekly sessions he embarked on a process of self-discovery, which was much more intense than during the first phase of our work together. He was open and curious to discover more and more about himself, probably under the pressure of his impending death. He made important discoveries and became very knowledgeable about himself. We stayed in touch until the end: Gerry was taken to a hospice; I visited him there. We spoke on the phone once a week until Gerry decided that he was suffering so much physically that he could no longer speak with me. We said goodbye. During the final days of the illness Gerry was sent home to die. His mother came to his home to care for him there. He died within a few days, two years after John.

Gerry's voyage of self-discovery was unique in my practice. I had never worked with someone who knew that his or her death was imminent. The fact that we had known each other before was helpful for the process. Gerry could be very open with me, confident in my reliability, in my being able to be there and to hold him in a way that was good for him. This second phase of our work was concerned not with some kind of crisis in the outside world, but rather with the preparation to meet death, the eternal foreigner whom none of us knows and we all, in general, fear. Gerry wanted to be able to accept the inevitable and fast approaching end of his life. Allowing himself to become more intimately acquainted with himself, who he had been, what his life had been, what made him up as a person gave Gerry a feeling of completeness, which I believe helped him to be able to pass. I think of him often, and am sad to think that if he had contracted AIDS today, he might still be alive.

Lisabetha's life

When I met Lisabetha she was 18 years old and had just finished high school: she was a lovely looking young woman who smiled all the time. We saw each other for a few sessions before she left for a year of volunteer work with a religious group devoted to helping better the situation of the people in a village in a third world country. A while after her return we started work together. Her smile had disappeared: she had had some very unsettling – even traumatic – experiences in the village and she had, unfortunately, not been well supported by the agency, which had sent her there.

We took up our work together again. It took Lisabetha a long time to be able to recount what her childhood had been like and it was only many years later that she allowed herself to realise that she had most likely been an unwanted child. Her parents had already had five children when, suddenly, at the age of 45, her mother was once again pregnant. The decision to keep the baby was difficult: her mother was already over-extended, taking care of the children, the household and her part-time job as a secretary in a very demanding international company. Her father was working most of the time in a very lucrative profession, devoting his free time to his buddies. He was very worried about the family's financial situation although he was already very well off.

Just after her birth Lisabetha was taken along everywhere – even in a backpack on her parents' cross-country skiing expeditions. When she was a little girl, her siblings had already left home; whenever her parents decided to go out at night, she was left alone at home. She was very afraid, but this did not interest her parents. Her cries and pleas fell on deaf ears. The parents showed little empathy for any of their children: they demanded complete compliance and had a strict code of values, which included being polite, courageous, honest, obedient and submissive at all times. These demands originated in the parents' own childhoods: both had been sent to boarding school at a very early age. Being sent away, abandoned by their own parents so early, they learned to ignore their feelings, which subsequently were never recovered. Feelings were foreign to them, dangerous, and to be avoided at all costs. Lisabetha learned her lesson and smiled as often as possible in order to signal to her parents that everything was all right; she was intent on pleasing, trying very hard to be liked and feel accepted. In order to achieve this, she needed to demonstrate how independent and capable she was. Only sometimes, like when she was left alone, did she have emotional moments, which were disapproved of and punished accordingly.

Lisabetha was treated very harshly when she did not comply. No mercy was shown. For the slightest wrongdoing her parents would threaten to call the police, to send her to jail; they locked her up in the cellar when she did not feel like eating the meat that was served for dinner. Lisabetha lived in constant fear. With time we managed to retrieve these memories; they had been well concealed, as they had been too painful to retain and challenged the image of good parents, which Lisabetha had always desperately tried to hold on to. But these experiences often surfaced in dreams, actually nightmares, which Lisabetha brought to our sessions regularly.

Lisabetha was also bullied at school; she was singled out as an outsider, as someone who did not belong to the crowd, just as Gerry (seen above) and Charles (to be discussed below) had been. For all of these three clients, feeling different and rejected had been a fact of life in their infancy; they had been unwanted and/or mistreated at an early age. Not only the "gleam in the mother's eye" was missing, but also the feeling of being accepted and belonging to the family. This exclusion was repeated in school bullying. But for Lisabetha, telling her father about the bullying sometimes got her a few sparing moments of empathy.

As an adult, Lisabetha felt tortured – as she had been as a child – but now she was being tortured by her own inner objects, the inner representations of her unempathic and severely critical parents. When, as a grown woman and recent mother, she realised that she was not complying with her original family's values, their cruel inner representations made her once again feel like the little girl who should be sent to jail for the slightest misdemeanour. Whenever Lisabetha caught herself thinking or acting differently from what her parents had expected of her as a compliant child, she felt them taking their revenge. She felt their reproaches as she had then, was convinced that she had committed some serious criminal offence, was really deep down inside a crook and had to be punished.

What brought Lisabetha the most relief and made her development beyond this stage possible was her discovery of the cook within. No, she did not cook with a grandmother. She, actually, had not had a loving grandmother. How did the cook get constellated? I believe it only became possible through our work together. I had often asked Lisabetha to write about her past experiences; my hope was that in writing she could come to accept what had happened to her, that she could then better digest these experiences and that with time her pain could be alleviated. Lisabetha enjoyed the writing and began writing children's stories with touching moral lessons, for example about learning how to be oneself. She then developed the desire to learn to draw so that she could illustrate her own stories. Drawing and painting became a passion for her; they allowed her to forget about her demons (as she called them) that accused her of so many wrongdoings and tried to crush her.

But, the conversion from her imagined life as a crook (going to jail for skipping school or not eating dinner) to cook was not spontaneous. It was rather the result of years of hard work. Lisabetha came regularly to our twice-weekly sessions over several years. The positive transference was extremely helpful. I liked Lisabetha and admired her determination to try to free herself from the demons of her past, to find a place in the world, to feel included in the world and not an eternal outsider. Lisabetha brought many dreams to our sessions and devoted many hours to writing them down and also recording what she experienced during our sessions. Sometimes our sessions were extremely painful for her. We worked with dreams, drawings, her physical reactions, the transference. We also worked with little objects that came to have strong symbolic significance for Lisabetha. The continuous reproaches of her mother – that she was acting too loud, too selfish, too cowardly – found a suitable image in a little bird cage with a little white bird in it: from time to time Lisabetha picked up the cage with the idea of locking up her condemning mother's reproaches and thus protecting herself from the continuous scolding. We discovered that it was quite miraculous that she had survived her childhood, as she had never found a positive supporting figure. We spoke of a guardian angel who must have been there watching over her. A little gold angel figure became her constant companion. She would invoke it in moments when she felt in need of support. The various little objects with which Lisabetha worked during our sessions were concretised images with an emotional power that surpassed, went far beyond and were more effective than images merely evoked in the imagination and described verbally.

I am including here, with Lisabetha's permission, a drawing of how she imagined the torturous situations of her childhood (Figure 5.2).

She represents herself as the tiny figure at the bottom of the image, being crushed underfoot by the demon – a tall, thin stick figure in stiletto heels, no meat, no tangible body – an animus figure of her mother, or a super-ego figure of both her parents. Lisabetha shows herself again, this time as a little, more ample figure on the right-hand side of the page; she has no real, usable hands or feet. Across her neck she has drawn lines to show how the reproaches are choking her. "Bad", "Liar", "You'll see!", "Shame on you!", the demon says in German, pointing its long, skinny fingers at Lisabetha and finally crushing her underfoot.

This is the way Lisabetha had experienced her life as a child: any misstep, any deviation from the family's norms or expectations was taboo. Lisabetha suffered throughout her life from these old memories and feelings that had been etched into her soul, internalised. Hers were not the dependable, caring, loving parents who held; her parents accused her of being bad, an outlaw, a crook who should be sent to prison. Lisabetha did, however, in the course of our work together, learn to develop in a manner that was far from the crook, actually its opposite. She became a cook, i.e. a creative individual who had her own personal way of

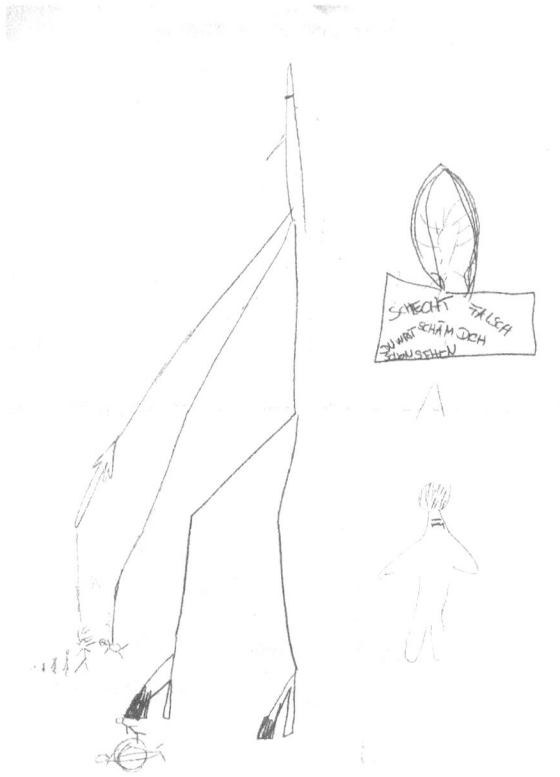

FIGURE 5.2 Lisabetha as a crook

seeing and thinking. With time she also developed a supporting and caring mother figure within, one who could hold her on her lap whenever the old well-known attacks made themselves felt.

The case of *"nomen est omen"*

The middle-aged man, very serious looking, with a brief case and thick eyeglasses entered my practice and introduced himself. He was suffering from panic attacks. A foreigner in the city, he had a contract to work here for two years. He had found my name on his consulate website indicating the names of therapists who spoke Dutch. My new client had a very unusual surname; I shall give him the name Duncecap here. Charlie Duncecap was born in Holland and spoke Dutch and English, but no German. It was of no surprise to hear that he had been mobbed in school because of his name, but the story of his early infancy did surprise me. He duly told me, and quite eloquently, what he knew about his early life, just as his mother had recently told him. At the time of his birth, his parents (who had immigrated to Holland from a country in Eastern Europe) lived in a large house in Holland. His father could not tolerate the baby's nightly crying. One night he was so bothered by the baby's crying that he smacked him several times (according to Charlie's mother, who divorced her husband when her three children were adults). From then on the father insisted that the baby be kept at the far end of the house where he and his wife could not possibly hear the baby's cries. This was done as requested.

Charlie grew up to be a strange little boy who often kept to himself. He was bright, even overly intelligent, but socially totally inept. He became a computer specialist with many quite obvious personal problems. To put it plainly, Charlie was a nerd, or what we in modern slang would call a geek. He was inept at social relations, but especially skilled in his technical field. He had no friends; his closest ties were with his siblings and his mother with whom he kept in close touch via telephone and especially Internet. In his new job, in a foreign country whose language he could not speak, he tended to keep to himself. He was not used to socialising anyway. His life consisted of work and cycling in his free time. What gave him special pleasure was drawing maps of places he visited, very exact maps that he created with the use of self-designed electronic systems that traced his pathways. Charlie was very meticulous about everything he did. This brought him a great deal of professional success and a great deal of fatigue.

During the night Charlie had very long, complicated dreams that sounded more like science fiction novels. He provided numerous footnotes to explain the pages and pages of single-spaced dreams that he had every night and kept track of with his usual diligence. His feelings of alienation from the world of humans, inhabitants of Earth, were reproduced nightly in his fantasies about foreign civilisations from distant planets in outer space that did not even belong to our galaxy.

Sometimes Charlie would arrive at our sessions, of which he never missed one, not knowing the time or date. He had tremendous fears of falling into an abyss. I recommended psychiatric help and he took antipsychotic medication regularly as well as continuing to see me. During one such session his fears were especially terrifying. Quite bewildered and also frightened that Charlie was having one of his episodes during our session, I realised that this was a good sign and a unique opportunity. By this time our relationship had obviously developed to such an extent that Charlie had some confidence in it and trusted me. I decided to try to take part in his experience in a rather unusual manner. I tried to adjust my voice so that it could be soft and soothing but also solid, not revealing the fear that I was feeling. I asked Charlie to try to describe the scene he was in, the landscape, himself, exactly where and how he stood. When I could well imagine where he was, after a while

I asked permission to join him, "What would it be like for you if I joined you there, at the edge of the abyss?" Charlie felt it could help him, so I went in my imagination and joined him there. And we stood there together. He was very frightened, but a bit less so with me at his side. I asked if in the fantasy I could take his hand. He agreed. We stood there together for a while, staring into the abyss, without saying anything. I was still quite frightened, but a bit less so, because Charlie had allowed me to join him. Charlie did not say much, yes, he did feel a bit reassured, not being alone at the edge of the abyss, not being alone to face the fear of falling or perhaps even jumping into the abyss to certain death. After a while I ventured to speak a bit more, daring to ask Charlie to accompany me – so that we could walk away together from the edge of the abyss. He consented. We retreated. He, and I too, felt relieved and we slowly stepped out of his fantasy world back to the reality of my practice room. He was no longer in the abyss state of mind; he was here with me and we were talking – very little – about reality. How was he going to spend the time when he left me? Did he feel like going to work the next day? Would he be speaking to his family? I needed to make sure that Charlie, despite his solitary life and the thousands of kilometres separating him from his family, would not be completely alone. I asked when he would like to come back for another session. He suggested in two days' time – that was more frequent than usual. It was a good sign.

Charlie's life had been one of extreme loneliness and helplessness in society. Our work was, I believe, successful because of the transference situation in which he was able, for perhaps the first time in his life, to develop trust in another human being. It goes without saying that his very early experiences in infancy, of brutality and abandonment, had destroyed his basic trust. In Jungian terms we can say that the ego–Self axis was broken. The ego was not able to be in touch with the Self, as the primal potential of and implicit guide for his development. Astonishingly, Charlie had many dreams that he could remember and gladly recounted. As products of the unconscious, Jung would consider them compensation for the conscious attitude, but they were actually a completion of the image of who Charlie was, lost somewhere in outer space and trying to find his way. We did not try to interpret the dreams, as I did not try to interpret the fantasy described above. We spoke of them: he shared his unconscious material with me, his analyst, and this sharing definitely fostered the development of the relationship. I believe also the fact that I, like him a foreigner in a foreign land, was able to communicate with him in his mother tongue, helped our bonding and contributed to Charlie becoming able to feel at home with me.

I must speak of the counter-transference here in which I, in the session in question, was drawn into Charlie's fearful fantasy of standing at the edge of the abyss. The extreme need to feel less abandoned, to feel accompanied in some comforting, reassuring way when in the grips of terror, doubtlessly stemmed from Charlie's early abandonment in infancy when he had been banished to the other end of the parental home, out of earshot of his parents. My counter-transference fantasy was provoked by his sense of urgency. My unconscious replied not with a need to interpret, but rather to enter into my client's fantasy world and reply with a reassuring hand. This is the contagion of which Jung spoke and which Jean Knox discusses in her *Self-Agency in Psychotherapy* (2011). Here she says that "an understanding of the developmental need for some form of enactment is precisely what enables the analyst to prevent this kind of extreme and severely damaging boundary violation". And, further on,

> ... the analyst's sense of being compelled is not necessarily a sign that a collusion is being demanded that should be resisted. The very experience of being compelled may indicate that there is a developmental need to relate, at least for a while, at the teleological level, through the use of indexical communication, in which the only thing that matters is the analyst's behavioral response.
>
> *(Knox, 2011: 117)*

I believe that through my counter-transference response, Charlie Duncecap was able to re-establish contact with a reliable, supportive function in him Self, which had been direly lacking in his everyday world from infancy onward.

Charlie, who had felt alienated since a very early age, actually probably since infancy, was a foreigner in a foreign land when he met me, also a foreigner in a foreign land. Perhaps it was also because of this similarity that I could become a helpful figure in Charlie's life. He could accept me when faced with the frightening fantasy described above and could allow me to accompany him in this moment of extreme despair. Being able to internalise this type of experience with a helpful figure would have been essential for Charlie's development. But my work with Charlie did not continue for very long. He asked to be transferred back to his hometown, where his mother and siblings lived. He felt more secure there.

The encounter with the numinous foreigner

In my analytical practice I have not often had the luck of being able to witness this type of experience. It is in fact unusual and very special. More likely are encounters with foreign aspects of the personality, which are surprising and often beneficial, but not as numinous as those which Jung himself experienced and described in his clinical work. The encounter I am about to describe here is a stunning (in both senses of the word) and exceptional case.

My client, whom I shall name Anna, did not undergo an instant transformational process; it took a great deal of time. But, one unique session and its contents did bring a huge developmental leap in the process. Anna originally came to me after several hospitalisations. She had a history of cutting herself and suicide attempts. No one had given her any hope of recovery; she had been labelled borderline (a diagnosis which I hesitate to use in any case, because it often means hopelessness). But at least she had not succeeded in killing herself. When she arrived for our first consultation Anna managed only with great difficulty to introduce herself and explain why she was coming to see me. She spoke slowly, haltingly, using very few words; she somehow did not seem to be quite present. A friend of hers, with whom I had done some psychotherapy a few years prior, had recommended me. Anna had just been discharged from the local psychiatric clinic; it was to be the last psychiatric clinic to which she would be admitted. She was in no way prepared to accept the fatalistic diagnosis that she had been given once again. She was determined to get better.

From the beginning I admired this young woman's determination. I was, however, concerned and worried about whether I really could help her. At that time I had a cute little dog who accompanied me in the sessions. In the presence of very disturbed clients he used to be very nervous and would bark so much that I had to take him out of the office. In this first session with Anna – as in all of the subsequent sessions with her – he was quiet and contented, snuggling up to Anna's feet, asking to be petted. I took this to be a serious sign of a possible positive prognosis. It gave me hope.

Our process was long and not easy. Anna always came exactly on time, never missed a session. She was extremely reliable. She often sat there opposite me without being able to say anything at all. When she spoke it was with great difficulty. What I realised with time is that she was trying very hard to find the best way to explain what was going on inside her. She was very imaginative and had a way of seeing things and explaining them more in images than in simple words; she often used the phrase, "as if … ". Anna had a very acute sense of symbols, which was a great advantage for our work.

With time she began reporting her dreams and drawing pictures of her dreams and fantasies as a kind of cartoon representation of her inner reality. The drawings were very expressive. Over time (a few years) Anna was able to remember the abuse she had regularly been subjected to in childhood – the beatings and ultimately also the sexual abuse by her father. This brought a major change. Anna seemed to be more present, more physically there. It was as if she could now stand on her own two feet again, balanced by her past and her present, both of which she was learning to accept as parts of who she was.

Among the many dreams, which Anna carefully noted and recounted to me, one was especially cruel and shocking. In it the numinous foreigner made its appearance. In this dream she was, as usual, being attacked by the members of her family of origin. This was a motif that we knew only too well. It had to do with the fact that Anna had not only had an abusive father but also a blind mother who helped in covering up the abuse. Without her complicity the father could not have abused the little girl again and again over so many years. Both parents indulged in alcohol abuse. Anna's siblings kept away from her as they had been told that Anna was not "all right in the head" because she had fallen as a child. The parents used this story to explain and conceal the real cause of the psychological problems the girl was suffering from: the father's abuse. In the dream in question here the members of the family seemed to be in the process of actually succeeding in destroying Anna completely. There was going to be nothing left of her at the end of the dream. I was speechless, as was she. I was both shocked and bewildered, not knowing quite what to do or say. Suddenly Anna stammered: "There is a blue lion … ". The unexpected entrance of an unknown mythical creature left us both once again speechless. Neither of us could say anything more than "how astonishing!".

In the subsequent sessions we indulged our curiosity about this creature and what it represented for her. She saw the lion as a lioness, actually a lion mother; for her and generally, this meant that the animal was protective, as lion mothers are renowned for their protective behaviour toward their off-spring. The fact that the lioness was blue made her just that much more magical. She was a special creature – appearing on the scene in the moment of the most extreme urgency, when Anna was in dire need of protection. It just emerged "out of the blue", as we say, to help her, actually to save her from complete disintegration at the hands of her family. This spontaneous creative moment – the creation of a hitherto unknown symbol from her unconscious – was a major turning point in our work. It was most likely the product of the critical moment of awareness of her impending annihilation in the dream – compensation, a lifeboat as she was falling into nothingness, being completely destroyed.

The blue lion was monumental and extremely strong; she had nothing else in mind than protecting Anna. It is actually not surprising that such a special mammalian creature was necessary to save Anna. She had not experienced a life-sized version of the protective mother in her own life. The unconscious provided the necessary being, but in bigger than life size.

Anna proceeded to give great care and attention to this autonomous symbol. She painted it huge on the wall of her living room; in her imagination it was her constant companion and of immense help in her everyday life in the world outside; it protected her from the destructive inner objects which her family had become and which had led her again and again to the edge of the abyss, to cutting herself and attempting suicide. She felt cared for, protected in a way that she had not known before. From this point on, under the auspices of the blue lion, Anna's life could develop and she could become the well-rounded person that she is today.

Jung often speaks of this kind of appearance of a symbolic creature as the appearance of the unknown third, uniting the conscious and the unconscious, offering a hitherto unknown, unimaginable solution. The blue lion was an utterly foreign being; it was so impressive and mysterious that it could in no way be ignored. It was monumental, not only in size, but also in significance. Anna's experience in the realm of the maternal had been disappointing: her mother's lack of care and attention had made it possible for the paternal abuse to occur and to continue for years. Anna had been lucky enough to have known – if only for a few years – a loving maternal grandmother. The presence of this figure in her life is probably what made it possible for a positive transference situation to develop. With time she could relax and feel safe and comfortable with me, as she had been able to with her grandmother. She could feel accepted and understood. On this basis Anna was able to commit to our work. We got along well together and could discuss difficult moments; Anna could tell me when she felt misunderstood. This was an extraordinary sign of trust in me and confidence in our work. I appreciated it. I felt comfortable with Anna and she with me.

Anna brought many dreams and was capable of accepting them and devoting to them the care and attention that made her unconscious feel welcome. Anna's numinous foreigner appeared on the scene to give her the monumental care, which she had been lacking. With this extra help, our work evolved to such an extent that Anna can today live a fulfilling life with a loving wife. She exercises a profession that gives her pleasure, has a circle of friends. Anna is one of the very lucky people who, having been abused by a member of her family, has recovered. The blue lion played an important role in her recovery.

The experience of her grandmother had made the potential appearance of a helpful inner figure easier to imagine, like a pattern that is laid out and is waiting to be filled out. We can call it a space saver for a helpful inner figure that can ultimately come and take its place. Anna's blue lion, as a foreign figure, became a helpful inner figure. Her imagination of the blue lion's presence in her life actually played the role of a helpful inner figure. The lion was hers, came to her to save her; she had imagined it, seen it, named it, painted it, and then took it with her wherever she went: it became her own inner helpful figure, the foreign being that entered her life and could be integrated.

And what about the analyst in the equation – a foreigner?

A large proportion of students at the institute for Jungian psychology where I studied in Zurich came from foreign countries. Many of us felt like foreigners during our studies in Zurich; this feeling foreign, not fitting in, not feeling accepted, not belonging to the surrounding Swiss society, and consequently feeling judged for not following rules we couldn't understand, feeling alone and isolated, criticised by some collective consciousness – such topics filled many hours of our training analysis. But I am sure these topics were only actualised through our Zurich experience.

Many of us graduates live and work today in places where we were not born or even spent our childhood. The fact is that the topic of foreignness, foreign identity and feeling foreign is a natural one for us. No matter where we happen to be practising now, those of us who left Switzerland are all faced with being seen by our colleagues in these new places as foreigners. Yes, we came from the Mecca of Jungian psychology, so we can perhaps feel special; on the other hand, we can feel embarrassed and defensive when the quality of our training is questioned by the local analysts. Where does the statement "I am a Zurich-trained analyst" take us?

How important is being a foreigner to the identity of an analyst?

The foreign analyst's perspective

I would now like to look at aspects and effects of the "foreign" analyst's perspective on the work. How does the experience of foreignness and the accompanying different perspective affect the work?

In *Memories, Dreams and Reflections* (1962) Jung remarks:

> We always require an outside point to stand on, in order to apply the lever of criticism. This is especially so in psychology, where by the nature of the material we are much more subjectively involved than in any other science. How, for example, can we become

conscious of national peculiarities if we have never had the opportunity to regard our own nation from outside? Regarding it from
outside means regarding it from the standpoint of another nation.
To do so, we must acquire sufficient knowledge of the foreign collective psyche, and in the course of this process of assimilation we
encounter all those incompatibilities which constitute the national
bias and the national peculiarity. Everything that irritates us about
others can lead us to an understanding of ourselves. I understand
England only when I see where I, as a Swiss, do not fit in.
I understand Europe, our greatest problem, only when I see where
I as a European do not fit into the world. Through my acquaint-
ance with many Americans, and my trips to and in America, I have
obtained an enormous amount of insight into the European character; it has always seemed to me that there can be nothing more
useful for a European than some time or another to look out at
Europe from the top of a skyscraper. When I contemplated for the
first time the European spectacle from the Sahara, surrounded by
a civilization which has more or less the same relationship to ours
as Roman antiquity has to modern times, I became aware of how
completely, even in America, I was still caught up and imprisoned
in the cultural consciousness of the white man. The desire then
grew in me to carry the historical comparisons still farther by des-
cending to a still lower level.

(Jung, 1962: 294)

I find it very interesting to note that Jung seems to be interested here in
other cultures because he feels that they help him to better understand his
own culture as a Swiss and a European. His perception of himself as a white
man is quite clear. He did, however, not realise the extent to which his attitude toward women and his understanding of the animus would make us
see him not only as a white man, but also as a white man of the nineteenth
century.

I actually wonder if feeling like a foreigner, having known what it is
like to feel one does not belong, is not a necessary prerequisite to becoming an analyst. Of course, as we have seen in the preceding pages, the
question of foreignness has many dimensions. The "outsiderness" of the
analyst can have to do not only with elements like nationality, religion,
language, culture, social class, sexual orientation and political views. As
analysts we also necessarily have a special perspective on things and are, in
some way, naturally outside of the society in which we live. Even on the
level of concrete reality many of us are outside of the society in which we
live. Because of the importance of the anonymity of our analytical persona

(requiring abstention and discretion) we generally take care not to belong to the in-group in society; we must be aware of and respect boundaries. We must try not to mix with the society in which our clients circulate, although at times this can be very difficult, especially when working in a small analytical community with our students, the on-going new analysts. We must keep a certain distance. I believe it is not an exaggeration to say, "This is the loneliest profession".

We can also find ourselves outside of the society because of having been brought up in a different culture, in a different religion than the majority of those around us. The foreigner is someone who has another identity than that of the place where he/she lives. But psychologically speaking, we can also sit outside. And this choosing to sit outside is important for our work.

There are many experiences of feeling foreign which I believe are beneficial for our work. Clients often come to us because they do not feel accepted within society. I shall come back to this in a moment.

We have seen in the second chapter how the fairy tale hero as an outsider often has the keys to unlocking the static situation. The analyst outsider with a different perspective is an important part of the analytic equation. A study on the topic of Latin American financial analysts found that their foreign analysts' performance was undoubtedly superior. The reasons: local analysts had conflicts of interest and tended to follow the crowd, whereas foreign analysts tended to have superior resources, better international expertise and even greater talent (Bacman and Bolliger, 2003).

This study might not be completely applicable for psychoanalysts. But there are some interesting points made, especially the idea of not following the crowd. We can take this to mean that as a foreigner one has a different, more independent perspective than the local analysts. An analyst needs to be able to have a different perspective.

All analysts have in some way known the experience of being a foreigner, of feeling like a foreigner or in some way an outsider. This foreignness need not be a question of travels. The necessary ingredient is, rather, the encounter with the foreignness of the unconscious. Our lengthy training analysis necessarily leads to the confrontation with the foreign in ourselves. On the level of personal life, one may also have known the feeling of not fitting in, be it in one's culture and even in one's own family, or just feeling different, as Jung says of himself in his autobiography from which we quoted in Chapter 1.

On the other hand, analysts also need to be able to empathise with our clients' needs for inclusion and their suffering from exclusion, their desire to belong, their insecurity, fear, frustration and anger at being excluded.

The opposite of foreign is familiar. The question of how much familiarity is necessary in order for a client to feel understood leads us to the transference, a topic of great importance for our work.

Some clients seek out their analyst because they are foreigners like them. They come with specific expectations: that I will be able to help them understand the foreign culture, that I will be able to understand the difficulties they are having in this foreign culture better than the locals with whom they associate.

And here things can become complicated. To be in the situation of living a special kind of relationship with the client is basic to our Jungian approach, but too close a relationship is also not desirable. The client who expects to be understood as a foreigner by a foreigner may show strong needs for relationship. We need to recognise these needs, empathise with them, but also to a certain extent frustrate them: this means being able to have one foot outside as well as one foot inside the relationship, an essential aspect of this complicated liaison.

In conclusion, it seems to me that all analysts are basically foreigners, or at least need to have known the experience in order to be able to understand our clients. On the other hand, we need to know familiarity, the sense of belonging and how important it can be, in order to empathise with these needs. Being too extremely focused on either pole does not allow us to experience or understand a larger scope of human nature. And of course dealing with the unconscious we need to be able to retain the excitement of the exploration with the curiosity of a foreigner.

References

Bacman, Jean-Francois and Bolliger, Guido (2003) 'Who are the Best? Local versus Foreign Analysts on the Stock Markets', *Fame Record Papers* 75. Geneva.

Jung, C. G. (1944/1952) 'Psychology and Alchemy'. *Collected Works, Vol. XII* (English Edition). Princeton, NJ: Princeton University Press.

Jung, C. G. (1962) *Memories, Dreams, Reflections: An Autobiography* (translated by Richard and Clara Winston; paperback 2019). London: William Collins.

Knox, Jean (2011) *Self-Agency in Psychotherapy: Attachment, Autonomy, and Intimacy.* New York and London: Norton & Company.

Marjasch, Sonja (1961) *Vom Ich im Traum.* Unpublished paper given to the annual meeting of the Swiss Society for Analytical Psychology in Berne. 9 July 1961.

POSTSCRIPT

This book has been the result of several years of study and reflection; it is a collection of unpublished essays on various aspects of the topic of the foreign/er. I hesitate to sew it all up and give a neat, clear picture of a topic that I feel is not at all neat and clear. Admittedly it is a ubiquitous and eternal topic and well deserves to be included in the archives of the archetypal world.

When asked by friends and colleagues after I submitted the manuscript why there is so much animosity toward foreigners today, I realised that I do need to express some kind of general opinion here.

First, I believe it is quite apparent that the extremely problematic attitude among many contemporaries toward foreigners is as old as mankind. In Chapter 2 I give examples from religious texts and other early cultures, which illustrate how complex and problematic the encounter with, and the presence of foreigners must have been in earlier times. I should also mention here that five of the Ten Commandments pertain to what one must not do to others. Who these others are is not specified. Based upon the evidence, if one may call it thus, of the Ten Commandments, one must surmise that people did exactly those kinds of things to others and as well as to foreigners: they envied them, took their possessions, their wives, killed them and "bore false witness" against them.

But there are definitely exceptional aspects to our era's xenophobia. It seems to be unusually widespread. The fact is that awareness about it is omnipresent. This awareness is due in large part to the media. There is hardly a place in the world in which the latest news about xenophobic activity anywhere in the world is not immediately reported via Internet, television, radio and newspapers. I believe that in early times xenophobic acts were not less widespread. The situation was perhaps even worse, with entire populations of foreigners being executed, entirely wiped out, because of the hatred of the established communities. We have been able to establish such facts for a relatively short time in history. Our historical knowledge of such acts of genocide is still relatively meagre. Modern media allow us to be aware of and follow these developments in a more immediate and efficient manner than ever before.

Another aspect of our present-day awareness of xenophobic ideas, speech and acts is an increased historical knowledge in people today, perhaps a result of the Shoah (otherwise known as the Holocaust). The horrific dimensions of its industrialised cruelty are known worldwide. It seems that there is not a secluded island anywhere on our planet that does not know about "the Holocaust". This knowledge seems to have made some people more sensitive and more aware of anything resembling this catastrophe. For this, education and the media are responsible.

Nevertheless, we are faced with shocking proportions of fellow men and women whose fear and hatred of the foreign/ers allows them to watch unmoved and to cheer anyone who tries to prevent the "invasion" (as this group calls the influx) of foreigners. News of attacks on schools, shopping centres, marketplaces, churches, synagogues and mosques, night clubs, immigrant shelters, innumerable deaths by drowning of people trying to escape from hunger and war, evoke no empathy among this sector of the population.

To what extent can the development of society and its effects on individuals help us understand the difference between animosity toward foreigners in the twenty-first century and the witch hunts, inquisitions and genocides of earlier times? What is the difference between this xenophobia and that of earlier centuries that burned women as witches and massacred non-believers?

It is often presumed that modern-day populations are more prone to shadow projection on minorities – scapegoating – because they feel less secure than earlier populations. It is true that we live in a time of extreme individualism. The structures and values of society, especially in the Western world, have become less rigid: norms have become lax; social mobility and widespread migration add to the disruption of societies that used to bind, but also hold their members. The individual's identity is no longer automatically granted by the society in which he/she lives. On the one hand, we have more of a sense of freedom, but also less security: freedom can be frightening; it can make people feel insecure. Among the basic – let us call them archetypal – human needs, one must include feeling that one belongs and that one is appreciated by society.

When society at large can no longer quasi-automatically offer people the fulfilment of these basic needs, these people can easily be seduced by groups like Scientology, Islamism and other sects, which round them up and indoctrinate them. Such groups definitely profit from this sense of insecurity, as they promise the fulfilment of those archetypal needs that people have been lacking in society. Terrorist groups feed on the phenomenon. Terrorist actions against foreigners generally stem from such deep-seated insecurities.

However, when we consider the constant wars of earlier centuries, the widespread incurable illnesses, the poverty and hunger, it is hard to imagine that people at those times felt secure. Yes, the Church and its values, the ruler and his laws, the relatively intact social structures did provide a sense of security that many of us today would no longer even consider a sense of security; we would rather consider them restrictions.

The archetypal model (analysed in Chapter 1) offers a possible way of understanding what is happening now. The model shows how scapegoating the foreigner can actually be a reversal, a flipping from one pole of the archetype to its opposite. Since at least the nineteenth century, travel to foreign countries has become a preferred pastime. The popularity of travel to foreign lands goes hand in hand with the popularity of foreign restaurants in one's own country. The aesthetically pleasing, the exotic, the fascination or at least the attraction of the foreign for its newness, its diversity is a prominent attitude in our world today. But, this appreciation can and does flip to its opposite! The best example of this flip, enantiodromia, as we call it, is Nazi Germany's attitude to Jewish people. The way the foreign and the foreigner are seen can turn into its opposite. The appreciation of exceptionally positive characteristics can easily flip from initial interest, even fascination to envy, hatred and the desire to eliminate the foreigner who has become undesirable. Fantasised monumental numbers of foreigners become threatening. Fantasised difficulties in communicating with foreigners can arise. These are all traits common to monsters.

In film and fantasy, monsters have recently become more approachable. Getting to know E.T., a creature from outer space in a film made over 30 years ago, made the characters of Earth in the film and in the audience empathise with E.T. and rejoice for him when he was able to go back home. Empathy is more likely when people sense similarities with others. Does the relatively recent portrayal of loveable, loving monsters give us hope for the future: can we really – as societies – try to become acquainted with foreigners and appreciate their humanness, their similarity to us, despite a need to utilise them as fields of projection, as scapegoats? Projection of the shadow tends, on the individual level, to be a less murderous phenomenon than on the collective level. Is it really avoidable on the level of the collective? Cultural complexes can be made conscious; in this way collective consciousness can be modified. Dealing with the foreigner in a more humane fashion might sound too idealistic. But, to quote Cicero: "*Dum spiro spero*" – "While I breathe, I hope". It is in this spirit that I have written this book.

Addendum

I had just completed the above Postscript when two events moved me to such an extent that I need to add some remarks here. First of all, around the corner from where I live and practise a rabbi and his two sons were spat at and verbally attacked. This shocked me: the problem is not far from home, in fact it is very close by. What this means for the Jewish community in Germany is not yet apparent. It is, however, part of a recent increase in anti-Semitic activity here. Like the current anti-Hispanic, anti-Black, anti-immigrant, anti-Muslim activity, it is alarming. Thus far, it seems that a majority of contemporaries who are neither Jewish, nor Hispanic, nor Black nor Muslim also find it alarming.

The second experience: a woman whom I met at a party, on hearing about my book, asked me if it was fiction or non-fiction. I was quite taken aback and could only answer, "Oh, … fiction? I wish it were!"

I find this an appropriate ending to my Postscript of August 11, 2019, over 2,000 years after the destruction of the first and the second temples in Jerusalem, events that ultimately led to the diaspora of the Jewish people.

INDEX

Locators in *italic* refer to figures/illustrations

For Product Safety Concerns and Information please contact our EU
representative GPSR@taylorandfrancis.com
Taylor & Francis Verlag GmbH, Kaufingerstraße 24, 80331 München, Germany

www.ingramcontent.com/pod-product-compliance
Lightning Source LLC
Chambersburg PA
CBHW070351270326
41926CB00017B/4091